CW00665926

1

DEDICATED TO THE MEMORY OF
Xochil "Zack" Vincent Fortune

ACKNOWLEDGMENT

Curtis Dupree - I would not be the man I am today without you. You are always on my mind, in my heart, and at the forefront of my walk.

Melanie Villegas - For the freedom you gave me to reject the world and pursue a life of purpose.

Erik Braden - For believing in us and becoming part of our family.

Ed Jordan - For your teaching and mentorship in my sales walk.

Al Brown - For showing me how to build anything.

David Massover - For guiding us with your wisdom.

James Carbary - For being an amazing friend and our biggest advocate.

Steven Kazmarcyk - For all your love and support.

Rich Johnson - For helping me #ChangeTheGame.

Andy Kelly - For your unwavering friendship and support.

Rick Bommelje - For taking the time to listen.

Rafael Barretto - You're a wizard and this book would be empty without you.

Beth Pagano - Your commitment, passion and dedication are the epitome of a true Rebel's heart.

SPECIAL THANKS

KT and Chan - Our partners in crime and our best support.
Carter, Trip, Izzy and Atlas - May this book make you proud
one day.
To our Familia - Thank you for your love and support, you
are our everything!
The Rebel Fam - Let this be a testament to the
power of community and the service you've given.

How to Start a Sales Rebellion

The Copier Warrior's Guide to Sales + Life...

WELCOME TO
THE SALES REBELLION!

This Rebellion began many moons ago with The Copier Warrior's Legend, in a distant land, far below the clouds. His journey would take him through some of the darkest valleys, and atop the tallest mountains. He is a conqueror of false sales professionalism, has made more sales calls than any auto-dialer could dream of, and ate copious amounts of tacos along the way. He bleeds toner and sweats integrity. He is Dale Dupree.

A rising outcast attempting to save the traditional sales cycle, The Copier Warrior sought to impact everyone he encountered. His sales practices and workflows have been locked away, hidden from the public eye, until now. This book is a curation of more than a decade of his works. More than that, it is a proclamation towards forging a charter forward to a new world for every sales professional. This is how The Copier Warrior became the leader of the Sales Rebellion. And, if you choose to go forward, understand that you are beginning your quest to become a Sales Rebel.

Service... community... excellence... all forgotten, all betrayed. They've become the enemy of the Sales Empire that rules from on high. Yet, these are the Principles behind The Copier Warrior's methods. These methods were dismissed by his peers and suppressed by the sales elite. His clients, however, along with manufacturers and industry leaders, recognized him for his great works and his record-shattering sales walk.

Thus, the pages set forth before you are sacred... the methods contained in this book can undoubtedly elevate your existence as a sales professional. However, true success is always conditional. Either you apply it from front to back and live by its core, or you take from these texts partially and forgo the Legend that could have been.

In the end, The Sales Rebellion believes that every person is a Salesperson. Teachers sell subjects, leaders sell a vision, brokers sell networks, and buyers...Well, buyers sell themselves.

Time is the currency and attention is the exchange.

THE SALES REBELLION
BELIEVES THE SACRED
PRINCIPLES LEARNED
WITHIN THESE PAGES,
WHEN IMPLEMENTED
WITH *TRUE SERVANT
LEADERSHIP*, HAVE THE
POWER TO *CHANGE THE
FUTURE* NOT ONLY OF
YOUR PROFESSION BUT
OF THE ENTIRE WORLD.
SIMPLY PUT...
THE WORLD IS IN DIRE
NEED OF A *REBELLION*.

HOW TO USE THE BOOK:

- Read one "Day" every day
- Read this book on the weekends as well ... A Rebel lives 24/7
- Each "Day" has a Challenge — Do. Them.
- "The Warrior's Words" are straight from the Copier Warrior himself and will help you build out a deeper understanding at the end of each weekday.

Beyond that, here are some additional details and suggestions that will help you make sense of everything you're about to encounter:

- Build a routine around the book — Spend time every day (preferably the morning)
- The first day is about doing first things first
- The rest of the first week covers what people think they know about sales
- Everything else is about the Sales Rebellion Philosophy and redefines sales as it is known
- Each day has a focus (i.e. prospecting, information gathering, etc.)
- Each day has 3 counterparts in the book (see contents and index)
- The weekends are an introspective approach to Self-Development

At the end of this book, you will not only have gained the mindset of a Rebel but you'll also have changed your professional outlook forever. Be open to trying new things and think carefully about where the sales industry is headed. What are the skillsets for a sales professional in the digital world? What is the added value of a human connection? Why is a Rebellion our best way forward?

NOTE TO SALES MANAGERS:

Our goal is for you to maintain high energy teams that are crushing life.

But know that it starts with you...

You have to be willing to experiment with a fresh set of ideas.

You have to be willing to empower sales reps to feel more pride in the process.

You have to create a culture that values impact and personal experiences.

Allowing your sales team to implement these ideas will not only increase the success(es) of individual contributors but allow for retention and recruitment like you've never seen.

This is bigger than a sales method... It's a Sales Rebellion.

Join it... or, get left behind.

THE WORLD OF THE SALES REBELLION

GLOSSARY:

Some terms you'll see throughout the book are nuanced to The Sales Rebellion (TSR) and deserve some explanations:

R.E.A.S.O.N. - It's the foundation of every first touch that salespeople should be making when prospecting. It's a radical way of engaging your prospect and creating undeniable curiosity through interrupt marketing.

Roots - This is your sales foundation. Only after you have truly planted your Roots firm into the soil will you be able to translate your Legacy. Through each interaction, you build unfettered authenticity and deeper relationships within your community.

Sales Wanderer - The mindset of one who travels their territory with purpose and intention. It's an understanding that the people behind the doors you knock on are looking for something greater than mediocre. The Wanderer is curious, knowledgeable, and eager to explore.

K.N.O.W. - This term represents the 4D vision at the pinnacle of understanding. It's about learning what's most important to the prospect and being able to apply the most intentional approach. These are the street smarts and 21st-century tools that create a successful sales career. K.N.O.W. is Knowledge, Networks, Orchestration, Wherewithal.

Living Pipeline - Forget what you know about a pipeline. Yours is old, rusted and leaking. We'll show you how to create a new one. One that is alive.

Chest of Wonder - Prospecting tools are more than business cards, brochures, white papers, and telephones. We'll show you how to create your own collection of interrupt marketing tools that will last throughout your entire sales career. These tools are not only trash-can resistant, but they also cause undeniable curiosity along with buy-in from your prospects from the first touch to the close.

CB-1-2-MANY - CB stands for ChatBot 1-2-MANY because you are one of way too many. But it's not your fault because this is what you were taught to do. CB-1-2-MANY is a representation of how all "salespeople" sound the same. Don't be a robot. Be a Rebel.

Xochil (Pronounced: Social) - We chose this adaptation in memory of a special friend whose bold spirit commanded the attention of those around him through authenticity, a special love for life, and ferocious creativity. Xochil Vincent Fortune — A.K.A. Zack, A.K.A. DJ Furoche — lived life fully, a concept that, although not directly stated, is inherently expressed throughout this book. Zack, in his infinite creativity, brought Jeff and Dale back together through his passing from this earth and is one of the reasons you're reading this book. We love you eternally Zack.

A NOTE FROM THE COPIER WARRIOR

To all of you who have uncovered my writings and are reading these words, please understand before you go any further... I used to suck at sales. Like, really bad.

When I first got started in my career I thought I had it all figured out, but quickly realized just how lost I truly was. No real system, no impactful habits, no true accountability, no idea what I was doing.

I definitely felt like a failure as my grandfather was a sales Legend and my father, his descendant. Who was I? Let me tell you... I was not very bright when it came to my products and services.

I was so focused on closing everyone I met that I forgot to bring my integrity to the appointment. I would constantly tell my prospects "Yeah, I think the new machine does that!" And, "It'll be about the same price that you're paying now." Or even, "We can have the machine here tomorrow if you'll sign today!" When in reality, none of those things were really true. I struggled with building rapport, I had a hard time thinking outside the box, everything was robotic to me inside my sales presentation. I was broke, no future in sight, no real plan, down on myself constantly, didn't think I was cut out... I was plagued by doubt and negative thoughts.

My dad was the light in my darkness. He would constantly tell me to stop treating everyone like a signature for my paycheck. People have needs and rushing to the finish line is not helping them. My dad helped me to humanize the sales cycle. He helped me to see the real roots I needed to grow, for myself, in order to be a successful salesperson. He taught me how to treat my prospects like friends, my territory as a community, and to see the bigger picture in building my Legend.

Determination and Empathy are the two words that defined my progress out of my old ways and into The Copier Warrior. Understand that what you see today is the product of my failure.

Years of failure. These writings are not about my success, they are about my experiences and every little thing I did to conquer them. All the while building a system around what I was learning.

Furthermore, these words, on these pages, were created in order to help you start writing a new chapter in your own story that will defy the expectations of the business world and the limitations you have placed on yourself.

A light switch flipped for me and it will for you too, because inside these pages is that same awakening waiting for you. I leave the decision in your hands as to whether or not you will flip it, as I did, and join The Rebellion.

Core Values:

CHOOSE LEGENDARY

The Pursuit of Excellence in all endeavors - personal, professional and private

CREATE WONDER

Making the human experience the primary objective at every level

SERVE OTHERS

Servant Leadership for all people in all things

CHANGE THE GAME

To reject the status quo and relentlessly pursue creative innovation

Our Mission:

CHANGING THE *STEREOTYPE* OF SALES THROUGH *CREATIVE* SALES OUTREACH AND *COMMUNITY* MINDED SERVANT *LEADERSHIP.*

TABLE OF CONTENTS:

LET'S GO...

DAY 01

R.E.A.S.O.N. AND YOUR ROOTS

RALPH WALDO EMERSON

"Don't say things, what you are stands over you the while, and thunders so I cannot hear what you say to the contrary."

Today, on your first day, we're going to introduce you to two of the Sales Rebellion's most fundamental concepts — Roots and R.E.A.S.O.N. This is where we create a foundation to build from. Roots and R.E.A.S.O.N. are, in essence, about understanding your sales walk, telling your story in a relevant way, and connecting with your prospects on a more meaningful level.

Let's start by defining your Roots. In sales, as in life, it's critical to understand that your words can move mountains. So think of your Roots as the foundation of that voice. In other words, the only way a prospect can ever know the value of doing business with you is if you learn to communicate it to them clearly. This means understanding the bigger picture behind your sales walk and having goals that are larger than closing a deal or making it to the two million dollar club. Understanding and articulating this concept will open the locked doors you have unsuccessfully been pulling on.

Today is designed to briefly introduce you to the concepts within Roots and R.E.A.S.O.N. We will cover each of these more in-depth in the days to come. Let's start by outlining your personal bio in a context that will complement the corporate brand you represent. This will help you to truly communicate your difference and value to those who are on the outside looking in. It'll take some time, and it should constantly be evolving, but you will begin to see its value as soon as you implement it.

As an example, let's share with you the fable of Keku the "Office Kahuna"...

Keku, like so many other CB-1-2-MANY, would quickly run down a bullet-pointed list when people asked him to share a little bit about himself. He would say that he was born in Hawaii, lived in Las Vegas, worked in politics, sold used cars, and has a family that he loves more than anything. But, this statement hardly does justice to who and what Keku really is. Furthermore, this type of statement does little to engage the listener and create a connection with them.

Here is what emerged from deep within his soul after starting his own Sales Rebellion, using the Roots and R.E.A.S.O.N. methodology.

Who am I?

I'm a local boy from the North Shore of Oahu who grew up in Las Vegas, Nevada. I graduated from UNLV (Go Rebels!) with a political science degree and had the opportunity to work in politics. Currently, I'm a technology consultant with HGI Technologies, a really cool company that's been around for 96 years! I absolutely love what I do. My position gives me an opportunity to interact with clients and to help them with their specific needs — primarily connecting them with office hardware and software that will help them save time, money and gain peace of mind!

I was blessed to have had mentors in my life who instilled in me the spirit of Aloha and Ohana. There are some of you who may ask, "what the heck does that mean?" The spirit of Aloha is an ancient Hawaiian concept that stresses kindness and respect. Ohana, on the other hand, is the Hawaiian word for family. In essence, that means, I'll always treat you with kindness, respect, and more importantly, like my own family!

To have effective interactions with prospects you must unite your purpose, mission, and self in a cohesive manner. This is how you add value. This is how the prospect begins to understand why it's worth knowing you, and better yet, why it's worth buying from you.

With Keku's newly defined Roots we feel like we understand who he is, not just what he does. We understand a little more about his culture and what we can expect by choosing to start a business relationship with him.

Simply put, one does not build credibility by being an "expert" in their respective industry. That's why your prospect gets three bids every time the contract is up for renewal. Furthermore, there has to be a reason for the individual you're interacting with to give you any form of trust. What better way than to be vulnerable and honest by sharing your heart and giving them more substance — not just a sales cycle full of features, advantages, and benefits.

Now that you have a brief overview of understanding and articulating the Roots of your Rebellion, let's talk about the R.E.A.S.O.N. theory and how to use it within your Sales Rebellion.

R.E.A.S.O.N. STANDS FOR THE FOLLOWING:

R.E. - Radically Educate: This is the first touch before any type of phone call/email/handshake with your prospect. We call it a first-touch piece (FTP). We'll talk more about how to create effective outreach later. For now, just know that it's a way to cause undeniable curiosity. This makes the prospect *want* to hear more about the R.E.A.S.O.N. you're reaching out.

A. - Attention: Think about the way you communicate your current 30-second commercial or elevator pitch. Now, forget about it... The R.E.A.S.O.N. method is an interrupt that stays consistent with your FTP and continues the prospect down their new adventure with you.

S. - Story: This is where you start throwing glimpses of the buyer's journey and your own tale into the conversation. This approach is based on the psychological effect that a story has on the person listening. It causes them to let down their guard and builds credibility, as well as helping them connect with you. This helps the prospect to open up and share more than, "yeah we have that product you sell and we're happy, thanks for calling."

O. - Outline: We jump "back to business" in this final piece of the process as we bring it all home. The idea here is to set yourself up for success by obtaining agreement from the prospect of the vision you both would like to see fulfilled. This is accomplished by focusing on service and building a deeper relationship with the prospect from the beginning. Never forget that you might even end up "being friends" and becoming referral partners if they don't qualify for your services.

N. - Nuance: This is the thread that weaves your R.E.A.S.O.N. together. The idea is to throw tiny glimpses of yourself throughout the "pitch" that you develop. Be human, be real, be yourself — NOT a CB-1-2-MANY.

So, why go through all this trouble to make an elaborate process just to pitch someone for an appointment?

The first reason is quite simple; the value of a good first impression. Beyond that, it's because most introductions are cut-off around 10 seconds. Way before you're done speaking, the person on the other end has either made up their mind they're curious to hear more, or decided they're not interested. They might be polite and let you finish your 30-second pitch, but they've definitely created a perception of you long before you're done.

Why? Because your pitch sucks and they've heard it all before. Your decision maker has become desensitized to salespeople because they're constantly bombarded by the same generic sales pitch. So articulate your R.E.A.S.O.N. with them and #ChangeTheGame.

Radically Educate those you interact with through an appetizing first touch. Then, utilize storytelling methods to build credibility and, in turn, have them open up to you about themselves and their business. This is the way.

Whatever you do, please don't fool yourself into thinking that focusing on the prospect's obvious and surface level information is a good way to break the ice — who are you to them in the first place? A stranger. That is a fact. So, telling the prospect all about the "widget" they create, where they graduated from college, or any other surface-level facts will *NOT* earn you the desired seat at their table. These can be seen as a "sales tactic" rather than true human connection. R.E.A.S.O.N. is all about going one step further: creating familiarity, causing curiosity, being relevant, and taking your prospect on an adventure.

To summarize... Does the surface level info help you get an appointment? Sometimes.

Does it build a relationship with your prospect? Get you invited to Thanksgiving dinners, Christmas Eve parties, firstborn baptisms, or secure a comfortable sales cycle? Definitely not.

To summarize, your Roots are important because they are the foundation of your Sales Rebellion and the success that follows alongside it. Your R.E.A.S.O.N. is important because this is how you express yourself, attract your audience, and engage with people beyond the surface level.

TAKE A FEW MOMENTS AND REFLECT ON THE QUOTE AT THE BEGINNING OF THE DAY...

TODAY'S ADVENTURE

Create your mission statement — make your audience believe that you're not just another CB-1-2-MANY programmed to talk fast and sell at all costs. Help us understand what drives and defines you. Why do you get out of bed and go to work every day? Tell your story and the story you want your audience to lean into. Then, share it with at least one person — stay cognizant of how you're presenting it to others and understand the purpose is to draw others in through familiarity while building credibility. "Finesse your pitch" as The Copier Warrior likes to say. It should feel like a natural conversation.

_____
_____
_____
_____
_____
_____
_____
_____
_____
_____
_____
_____
_____
_____
_____
_____
_____
_____
_____

THE WARRIOR'S WORDS:

I can still remember my first day in sales. I was lost, confused, and extremely excited all at once. My father was a great teacher and knew the best way for me to learn was to hit the streets and fall flat on my face. It's one of my fondest memories, as weird as that might sound! The Roots I firmly planted along with the R.E.A.S.O.N. I developed were cultivated by my actual experiences. It was my beginning. This is how I became The Copier Warrior.

Ultimately, I came to believe in relationship selling and humanizing the sales process. The goal behind this practice is to help those you seek to serve see past the suit and tie, or the products and services. You want them to recognize the outstanding and genuine human-being standing before them.

Remember, being an "expert" is table stakes and has become a requirement in this modern age. All of your competitors are also "experts." Being an expert does not make you different. So head to www.TheSalesRebellion.com to learn more about some of the programs that will help you differentiate yourself and sharpen your Roots and your R.E.A.S.O.N.

Ask yourself a question: Am I creating a meaningful impact and living my most Rebellious life with my existing pitch? Or, am I just another number in the crowded bullpen?

DAY 02

TERRITORY PART 1 A NEW APPROACH

NAPOLEON HILL

"There is no scarcity of opportunity, only scarcity of imagination."

It's time to rethink your territory as a true Rebel. Every salesperson lives or dies by the community they serve. So let's dive deep and break it down, piece by piece, just as The Rebellion has called us to. Most people see their territory defined by boundaries like zip codes and interstates. They see it as the yellow highlighted area on the map in the office. So, today, we ask you to reimagine your territory. For this, we want you to draw a circle.

Now, imagine inside of that circle are highways and backroads, retail shopping centers and industrial parks, small private practices and big corporate headquarters. Picture the highways and backroads as hiking trails, private practices as a calm waterfall tucked away, and corporate headquarters as small mountains to climb along your journey. The key here is to visualize your territory in a much less threatening or generalized way. It should be a land of adventure and wonder, a land of detailed nuances and cultural diversity, not a bunch of meaningless lines and mile markers.

This commences the start of a journey into your territory. We offer this insight in hopes to change your perspective and give you guidance that cultivates a deeper understanding of the opportunity that your territory holds.

So, let's discuss what's inside your territory.

OFFICIAL DISCLAIMER:

These averages and examples are taken from the copier industry and will vary depending on your vertical and marketplace.

In most sales verticals, you will be given a territory with a list of prospects that reside within. Most verticals will also label prospects in regards to the size of the opportunity and type of transaction. For example, let's say your territory has 3,000 viable accounts (viable accounts represent a 30% portion of the total marketplace) and those opportunities range from A to C:

Here is how the Sales Rebellion defines A, B, and C accounts:

- Your typical A account is perceived as a "major" win and would be worth a higher revenue amount than any other account type
- Your standard B account is perceived as an "above average" win and would be worth a mid-range revenue stream
- Your average C account is perceived as "transactional" because the rep is usually not worried about the long-game with this account. It is a very small win and only chips away a tiny piece of your revenue goals

Now, let's explore how most people approach building their strategy in regards to prospecting these 3,000 accounts. Once they have organized all the accounts into the respective A, B, or C category, they start to plan out their weekly calls. They map out 50 phone calls per day and 50 total in-person calls per week (10 per day). This equates to 300 "touches" inside of that territory on a weekly basis. Let's break it down in a simplistic manner using the example:

- 50 total calls per day (+10 in-person touches) = contact with 10 decision makers
- 10 decision makers per day = 2 appointments per day
- 10 appointments per week = 1.25 closable sales per week
- 1.25 closeable sales per week = 5 sales per month
- In summary, 50 calls a day = 5 sales per month

Now, let's talk about the numbers above in relation to the territory while focusing on income and time.

With the majority of accounts being B's and C's, reps will average $7.5k per sale and $30,000 in revenue per month. Average entry-level quotas (again, copier statistics) are $36,000 per month in revenue.

If a rep were to have the average results (as outlined above) in a territory with 3,000 prospects in it, they'll be selling $7,500 worth of goods and services to each account. When multiplied by the total number of accounts, the "worth" of your territory to you is $22.5m in revenue. That sounds rather nice!

So, let's say there is 25% of profit in each sale under these assumptions above.

$$\begin{array}{r} \$22.5M \\ \times\ 25\% \\ \hline \$5.625M \end{array}$$

If the numbers run true, you are looking at $5.625 million in profit for the firm you are representing. Now, let's look at these numbers with a compensation plan based at 30% for the rep.

$$\begin{array}{r} \$5.625M \\ \times\ 30\% \\ \hline \$1.7M \end{array}$$

If the average compensation plan pays 30% of said profit, you are looking at close to $1.7 million in total commission for the rep. No wonder people want to be in sales, right?

But, let's take a closer look at this...

If a rep makes 300 total calls per week, they can expect roughly 10 appointments per week, which boils down to an average of 5 sales per month... 5 sales per month means it will take approximately 600 months to sell all 3,000 accounts in your territory.

Now, 600 months is equal to roughly 50 years. So, that 1.7 million dollars spread out over those 50 years equates to an average commission of $34,000 per year to go along with whatever your base salary is.

What if you had to work your butt off and could have $1.7 million but only in $34,000 increments once a year for the next 50 years?

Makes you really want to be a salesperson, huh...

Makes you want to double down on your calls, huh...

In the end, $22 million in a territory is a great opportunity for a salesperson to have a very fruitful career. And, depending on what you sell, this might be a small number. However, when you break it down realistically based on an average day, translated into an average week, translated into an average month, translated into the average compensation program, these very sexy numbers quickly become very dissatisfying.

Now, take everything you know about your territory, as it has been described, put it in a little box, strap a grenade to it, and throw it into a deep dark hole that you will never look down again.

It's time to move on... abandon the average and Choose Legendary.

TAKE A FEW MOMENTS AND REFLECT ON THE QUOTE AT THE BEGINNING OF THE DAY...

TODAY'S ADVENTURE

- Rethink your territory, map out its worth and the A, B and C accounts
- Start breaking down your territory's worth, what your income goals are, and all the factors that come into play
- Start gaining a clearer vision of your sales career

_____
_____
_____
_____
_____
_____
_____
_____
_____
_____
_____
_____
_____
_____
_____
_____
_____
_____
_____
_____
_____
_____
_____

THE WARRIOR'S WORDS:

Spoiler alert as a rep I wrote an average of $1,830,000 per year (13 year average) in new business to an average of 74 net new accounts per year (13 year average) calling on less than 300 total accounts each fiscal year...

My average profit margin was 39% (13 year average) and my average commission payout was 45% on that profit.

My record in one month was 19 new accounts... 3x the "average" performance.

This is all about flipping the script on what people tell you is average and to better understand exactly what you can achieve.

Consider this as well: The average tenure for a B2B sales rep is between 18 and 36 months. Which means an average performance really truly doesn't pay off in the long run.

DAY 03

PURPOSEFUL PROSPECTING - BEHOLD, HUMAN INTERACTION

THEODORE ROOSEVELT

"Far better it is to dare mighty things, to win glorious triumphs, even though checkered by failure, than to take rank with those poor spirits who neither enjoy much nor suffer much, because they live in the gray twilight that knows neither victory nor defeat."

The question today is... why exactly do you prospect? Is it to zip through your "list" to make sure you've hit your 100 calls per day mark? Is it to update your CRM so you can show your activity to the boss, all the while crossing your fingers and hoping to find someone buying this month... If so, then you're not prospecting for the right reasons... and your activity is meaningless. As a Rebel, your intention behind prospecting should be to find opportunities in your community and expand your reach. This is the path in awakening your success through building relationships.

Your TPS reports and CRM activities don't make sales for you. On top of that, your prospects don't care if they're the 100th person you called today. Understand that nobody cares as much as you, that's the lesson here folks. All the "hard-work" in the world means absolutely nothing when you're blindly going through the motions, expecting it to magically produce results.

So, let's talk about purposeful prospecting and having the mindset focus.

When you were a kid, how did you introduce yourself to the people you met? How did you develop a friendship with them? You probably spent weeks, months, even years, developing those relationships. You built a culture of friendship which expanded into a community. Did you do it by shaking one of their hands and saying: "Hi, my name is Steve, and I am wondering if you have the three qualifying features that would make you a great candidate for being my newest best friend?" Maybe you did... But did it work?

No.

So, why do we do this every time we meet a prospect? The answer... because you look at them as a buyer... simple as that.

To make a long story short, every time you hear someone say "You have to make 50 calls..." you should cringe. Why don't you change your attitude in regards to the activity of prospecting? Why don't you Rebel?

Look at those 50 people as 50 different potential allies instead of a gauntlet to "yes." If you were prospecting correctly, you wouldn't be able to get through 50 calls a day. If you were prospecting correctly, you'd have quality conversations that lead to meaningful information you can then put in the CRM. That's the real bottom line.

So... dare mighty things, be vulnerable, get uncomfortable, and start a Rebellion! Your outbound activity will become the best inbound conversions you've ever experienced. It's time to build consistent prospecting habits using the principles of time management, and intentional interactions in order to take your sales career to undiscovered lands.

TAKE A FEW MOMENTS AND REFLECT ON THE QUOTE AT THE BEGINNING OF THE DAY...

TODAY'S ADVENTURE

- Re-focus your prospecting efforts
- Have conversations instead of pitching
- Take a handful of people from that list of 50 prospects and focus on what might catch their attention
- Allow yourself to develop a relationship that will inevitably turn into an opportunity
- For this adventure we want you to change your attitude toward prospecting... at least momentarily

THE WARRIOR'S WORDS:

Be cognizant of "the motions." I'm not saying your intentions are to go through the motions, or that you blatantly have the attitude expressed above. I'm saying that prospecting is not a "motion" we act on in order to keep our jobs and stay in good standing at the firm. Most people live in the gray twilight that knows neither victory nor defeat. And this, my friends, is why they have to make 100 calls on a daily basis. It's called "chasing your quota."

You're not finding success because you peeled off your human flesh, replaced it with CB-1-2-MANY armor, and left your heart and soul at the door when the clock struck 8:00 a.m. - A CB-1-2-MANY indeed. Prospecting takes discipline, confidence, a hard work ethic, a full heart, an open mind, and an objective that consists of service in its purest form. If you want to do 300 cold calls a week, to get 10 potential decision makers on the phone, to find 5 potential deals, which you'll probably lose (honestly), you'll have one heck of a terrible experience as a salesperson.

DAY 04

SERVICE ABOVE ALL ELSE

ROBERT F. KENNEDY

> "Each time a man stands up for an ideal, or acts to improve the lot of others, or strikes out against injustice, he sends forth a tiny ripple of hope, and... those ripples build a current which can sweep down the mightiest walls of oppression and resistance."

The path to becoming a Sales Rebel starts with the word Service. Is it an obligation... or, an action you gladly perform? Do you "serve" others because you want them to buy from you? Or do you serve from deep within your soul, without any expectations other than hoping to fulfill the void that traditional buyers feel? What about networking with other sales and business professionals? Are you giving freely without expecting a referral in return? Are you truly impacting your community as a Sales Rebel would?

It's important to ask yourself: What defines a "successful" sale? Is it winning with the cheapest price? Is it a favor for a friend? Is it a free iPad with your purchase? No. As a Rebel, it is fulfilling a need through an act of Service. It's the ground on which mutual interests meet, and cause an undeniable feeling of satisfaction for both parties.

A true form of Service sounds like this:

"I'm not sure my products are a good fit for your business. However, I will say it's my goal to be able to serve you in some capacity, even if that means sending you to another company that will better meet your needs. At the end of the day, I'm looking to earn credibility and some referral business, whether you buy from me or not. I'll tell you upfront I won't always be the 'cheapest' option, but I hope to translate true value in my actions today and going forward.

Understand that your career hinges on your attitude, and your attitude will define the way people perceive you. The foundation of a successful attitude is to be in it for the glory of those you can serve. Stop reading "service" in the old way you have understood it. Start practicing its definition: "The action of helping or doing work for someone without expecting something in return." Nowhere in there does it say "...so you can get rich quick to fulfill your financial goals and pilot a yacht by the age of 42."

Instill a sense of hope into your community and shine the light of your Rebellion.

TAKE A FEW MOMENTS AND REFLECT ON THE QUOTE AT THE BEGINNING OF THE DAY...

TODAY'S ADVENTURE

- Take the "I" out of your sales habits and start practicing service
- Deliver on a service-related task for your client
- Give a referral to someone on your prospect list
- Take a moment to write some of the countless ways that you can truly serve your prospects and clients today
- Take action and own this new way of thinking for yourself

_____
_____
_____
_____
_____
_____
_____
_____
_____
_____
_____
_____
_____
_____
_____
_____
_____
_____
_____

THE WARRIOR'S WORDS:

These 3 core statements helped to define this part of my sales walk:

- A Rebel is a friend, advisor, and Servant always, and a CB-1-2-MANY never.
- A Rebel is a leader with integrity and values as the root of my relationships with my prospects, clients, and co-workers alike.
- A Rebel is focused on the road less traveled and not the quick and easy shortcuts.

DAY 05
BEING IN THE K.N.O.W.

— OLIVER WENDELL HOLMES —

"A word is not a crystal, transparent and unchanged, it is the skin of a living thought, and may vary greatly in color and content according to the circumstances and time in which it is used."

You spend most of your upbringing doing some sort of school work with the intention of sharpening yourself through knowledge all so you can conquer the world. Or, at the very least, so you can get a job when you graduate. You use some form of knowledge to master a skill that you intend to use in the working arena, one you feel passionate about. Does it always work out? No. Some folks end up tilling the farm and milking the cows with a political science degree. The point is, you focus so much on "knowledge" as the world would have you see it. Rarely are you educating yourself in a manner that truly helps in the long run or labels you as a Rebel.

In a sales role, you apply your knowledge of products and services to hunt for potential buyers who need your widget. You meet with the customer and give them an elaborate presentation, you sell the sizzle and work the process. Then, a few weeks later, you get an email from the point of contact stating "we decided to go with your competition." Why?

It's because you barfed your sales pitch all over the prospect's table It's because you never allowed yourself to truly understand his/her business .It's because you never took the time to truly know their processes.

You only asked the questions that were important to your sales cycle to qualify your offering. You only wanted to get a "yes" and close a deal. Because of this, you're just a commodity; a price. And unless you're at the bottom of the barrel on said price, you lose.

Even with all the knowledge in the world, most salespeople continue to live in the status quo of mediocrity...

Just as you've been asked to completely revolutionize your first touch, your territory, your habits, your attitude... you're being asked to utilize the concept of knowledge to achieve that next level.

Being in the K.N.O.W. is about experiences, street smarts, and a real understanding that will help you to empathize and better serve your prospects' businesses. Get started with this process well before you make the first call. Educate yourself on the vertical, understand what types of businesses they serve, how many employees they have, and what each one's particular role and objective is. Don't generalize them into the traditional department buckets. Learn their name, shake their hands; ask, listen, discover their why and their mission. It's one of those things that's simple... but not easy.

You might know the general function of HR, but what's it like to be the HR department for a particular vertical, and how does your solution complement their daily habits? Better yet, what could your competition's product NOT be doing to complement their daily habits? The bullseye on educating yourself beyond the surface level internal functions of a potential client is to help make a more compelling case to them. This helps you articulate *why* they should listen to you. To build an emotional bridge that communicates credibility in its purest form.

This all ties back into the R.E.A.S.O.N. theory, along with your attitude of Service above all else.

If a buyer wanted to buy a copier to make plain old boring copies, to scan a few things here and there, or to print some emails every once in a while, then they wouldn't really value the copier, would they? So, they wouldn't really care if they bought it from you or Amazon. However, when buying online, they sacrifice a relationship for a cheap deal and they eventually have feelings of regret and anger toward said product. Especially when the 1-800 number puts them on hold for 90 minutes only to pick up and say, "please unplug the device and plug it back in."

Every company you touch is different. Stop generalizing your pitch. Start learning the language of your prospect. Endeavor not only to speak it fluently, but to serve their needs and help them achieve their mission and purpose.

TAKE A FEW MOMENTS AND REFLECT ON THE QUOTE AT THE BEGINNING OF THE DAY...

TODAY'S ADVENTURE

Commit to this idea of understanding your prospect better: Commitment leads to action, action leads to experience, experience leads to expertise. Go take the tour at one of the manufacturing plants in your area, go ask the local research clinic to learn more about what they actually do.
Go and experience. Take notes!

THE WARRIOR'S WORDS:

Understand that knowledge is more than power, it's a pure form of collective enablement in which your prospect is crowned King or Queen. This is the true identity of being in the K.N.O.W. You'll learn more about this theory in the coming days and get the opportunity to dive deeper into this subject. For now, know the most important kind of education involves sacrifice and an intentional attitude. Do not take lightly this form of learning, for if wielded correctly, it will reward you and those you seek to serve beyond measure.

DAY 05

DECISION... HAVE YOU MADE YOUR DECISION...

HENRY VAN DYKE

"What we do belongs to what we are; and what we are is what becomes of us."

Commitment is hard. It requires a definitive decision that there is no real coming back from. Once you commit, whether it be something small (like dinner for the evening), or something big (like marriage), there are tangible effects that will be felt both in the moment and throughout the rest of your life.

Most people take their everyday decision-making lightly and, in turn, put major emphasis on just a handful of decisions throughout a lifetime. You are to make a memorable mark on your community and the businesses you serve. But, you must put a major emphasis on your decision to join the Rebellion, and adopt the principles that made The Copier Warrior a Legend inside of the copier world.

You've been introduced to a wide variety of information over the last week. Was it what you were expecting? Maybe you didn't really want to get this deep. Maybe you were just hoping for us to throw a few sweet one-liners out there, or exaggerate how our way of email marketing is just so much better than anyone else's. But this is the Rebellion, and we're here to be honest with you. Thus, it's imperative to understand that without insisting on the importance of things like service, your community, and your purpose... we would be doing you a grave injustice, and everything in the pages of this book will have been for nothing.

Today (Saturday) is for reflection. Take a moment to look back on everything we've challenged you with: Will you walk the path of complacency and mediocrity, or will you commit to becoming a #Legend?

TAKE A FEW MOMENTS AND REFLECT ON THE QUOTE AT THE BEGINNING OF THE DAY...

TODAY'S ADVENTURE

Decide: Will you anwser the call of the Rebellion?
Sign here: _____
Date: _____
Who will you tell: _____

DAY 07
SELFISH, NO MORE

> ALBERT CAMUS
>
> *"Life is the sum of all your choices."*

In life, there is a choice of great relevance to our success. Although it can seem irrelevant at times, its effect on our future can be far more impactful than one could ever imagine. This choice is between service and self. It's easy to say "I serve because I will be rewarded," or "karma brings good things back around," but it takes a lion's heart to serve without expecting any form of reward. To serve for the sake of service.

We get it sounds more appealing when stated: "If you serve, you'll be given joys abundant in the form of continued success." And, while we believe this to be true, we also feel strongly this attitude can be selfish and often causes people to fall short of true service.

If your heart is full and your head is clear, your service will mean more. Think of service without recognition as a good example:

You're blowing leaves off your driveway... your neighbor is out of town - and you see a nightmare amount of debris piling up in their driveway... you clean it off for them without any desire of acknowledgment toward your work — this is a simple but true act of service.

Apply it to life, apply it to sales, apply it every day. Today (Sunday), is about service to your community beyond the workplace. We believe so wholeheartedly in service that we have a day devoted to giving back. Today, your day, this moment. Are you ready to lead?

TAKE A FEW MOMENTS AND REFLECT ON THE QUOTE AT THE BEGINNING OF THE DAY...

TODAY'S ADVENTURE

Give something away without recognition. Whether it be clothes to a dropbox, anonymously donating a few dollars to a charity, or just blowing your neighbors leaves off his walkway with a mask on so they don't recognize you — serve without expectations.

P.S. Please don't get arrested for trespassing on someone else's property while trying to anonymously do something nice for them...

DAY 08
FINISH BEFORE YOU START

HENRY DAVID THOREAU

"To him whose elastic and vigorous thought keeps pace with the sun, the day is a perpetual morning."

A morning routine or ritual should be a sacred thing. It should be something you connect with from a different perspective, on a higher level. Something familiar, something motivational, something that reminds you of the bigger picture and keeps you grounded to your Roots. Routines are all about discipline and focus, two key ingredients for a successful sales walk.

Let's kick thing's off with a few questions...

- How do you spend your time each day?
- Do you have a maintained schedule of personal habits?
- What about sales habits?
- Do you practice them daily/weekly/monthly?
- Do you know what we're talking about when we speak of habits?

As an example, think about the 8-5 routine that 99% of employed individuals practice on a weekly basis. You get into the office, you plop down at the computer, you answer some emails, you go through a list of "todos," you take a lunch break around noon, stop by Frank's office and chat it up with him about the new Star Wars movie, high-five the boss as he heads home early like he does every day. Then you shut things down around 4:45 and you're out the door by 4:59. Rinse and repeat tomorrow, and the next day, and the next... These are the typical habits of the working world... But not the world of a Sales Rebel.

Maybe this example suits your situation better: you hop into a collared shirt, spray stuff in your hair, and then angle the camera up so people can't see you're still wearing pajama bottoms. You run through your morning meeting, take a deep sigh of relief when you click that end meeting button, then look around wondering what to do next. You putter through a few calls before taking a long lunch in front of your favorite Netflix show... only binging two episodes today of course. Then you reschedule that last 4:30 call for tomorrow because, well, its been a rough day. Rinse and repeat tomorrow, and the next day, and the next... Again... not the life of a Rebel.

To fulfill the high calling of the Rebel, your morning habits should be centered around causing your own daily awakening. They should draw you in, excite and motivate you. They should keep your mind healthy, your focus on the end goal, and your heart full. Be intentional about creating an environment that supports the habits you want to create.

The first thing a Rebel does in the morning?

Goes on an adventure...
Remember, your daily attitude needs to be focused on how you're going to conquer the local/national/global market. Bring a sense of fun and excitement back to your morning rhythm.

Understand, everyone has a different routine they prefer to start their day with. Most Rebels spend about 45/60 minutes in the house *before* they even leave for work... Why? Because it's important to focus on self before heading out to serve and sacrifice for the benefit of others. Imagine, when you first rise out of bed, you head into your personal office space, the first thing you come in contact with is a quote... The Copier Warrior has two:

"My heart longs to learn and aches to serve."

"On the plains of hesitation, bleach the bones of countless millions who on the verge of victory sat down to rest, and while resting they died."

Remember, the aforementioned "office space" at the house should be full of motivational aesthetics: favorite movie posters, video game collectibles, LED lighting to set the mood, a "dream board" showcasing goals you are trying to reach, etc. These things serve as a daily reminder as to what you're seeking.

Next, turn on some music in order to further incorporate your personal life and the things you love into your workday. Music is a sensory pick-me-up and is one of the most powerful tools on this earth, wield it to your benefit! Allow the beat, the lyrics, the passion, the true meaning behind it all, to push you.

Another thing Rebels do is keep a journal. Journal anything that is on your mind, in order to permanently record your thoughts so that you can reflect on them later. Next, start a dialogue with your mentors, a prospect, or a current client that you're nurturing a more intimate business relationship with. It's early in the morning, so they're not going to necessarily be responding. However, it will be the first thing they see once they wake up and check their phone!

Once at the office, here's an example of the rhythm a typical Rebel would get into:

- Check the calendar and see what the day holds from all angles.
- If you have appointments, use Google Maps to find the address, then zoom out of the map and find businesses in the area you want to connect with in between your scheduled appointment(s). If there's a road nearby that you've never traveled, put it on the list. Not all who wander are lost!
    Note: if you work remotely you can literally still do this... Don't make excuses! Apply the concept above to far more than your digital world.

- Write thank-you notes to everyone you met with the day before and put them in the mail. Handwritten notes - they're more meaningful.
- Send any email follow ups that are currently on the table, and email any prospects you haven't spoken to in several weeks. Cultivate that relationship, baby.
- Before you start talking to people cold over the phone. PRACTICE!
- Put thought into your Top 10 or 25 Accounts for the day. Do your research! Think of new strategies if you're not already in the door. Think of ways to continue to develop the relationship. Write them down to implement. Go around the office and high-five the crap out of everyone.
    *Virtual high-fives if you work remote!
- Get the energy flowing, be the catalyst of positivity to the days — a leader in the eyes and hearts of your teammates
- Print out blank contracts for every single appointment you have — not because you're going to win the deal, or even sign anyone up... Do it because you are building an attitude of success.
- Do all of this before 8:30 am.
- Seriously. Do all of this before 8:30 am.

Look, not everyone wants to be up at 5:00 am and in the office at 7:00 am. Understand the outline is a structured mentality. If you're good, you can accomplish a whole heck of a lot between 8:00 am and 5:00 pm. When you're reaching toward unprecedented levels of success, however, your Legacy should not hinge on an eight-hour workday.

This type of attention to detail will help blur the line entirely which is what real Rebels do. So remember this — the clock is your ally and habits, over time, define the success you attain. Now go crush your day!

TAKE A FEW MOMENTS AND REFLECT ON THE QUOTE AT THE BEGINNING OF THE DAY...

TODAY'S ADVENTURE

Write down your habits (personal and professional) and execute them before 8:00 am. Create a schedule that empowers your day. Start at 5:00 am — not saying you need to be awake, but recognize that successful people have started their day at this time. So, if you're still asleep... dream of winning.

_____

_____

_____

_____

_____

_____

_____

_____

_____

_____

_____

_____

_____

_____

_____

_____

_____

_____

_____

_____

_____

_____

_____

_____

THE WARRIOR'S WORDS:

Understand that this is all about an attitude of willingness to better your current situation and serve the community in which you call home. Habits are important because they will evolve you into a time management machine, that teaches you discipline and focus. At the end of the day, we're telling you without structure and habits, you can never truly care about your own success. If you're in sales to make the base salary, and to barely hit quota... then put this book away — these habits are the core of your journey to Legendary.

DAY 09

TERRITORY PART 2 — A BETTER WAY, THE ONLY WAY!

ARTHUR YOUNG

"Give a man the secure possession of a bleak rock, and he will turn it into a garden; give him a nine-year lease of a garden, and he will convert it into a desert."

Welcome back to your territory. In our last visit to this sacred land, we discussed what it looks like to sell inside of your territory, and just how chaotic and unstructured this wonderful place really is. Then, we asked for you to take everything you know about it and sacrifice it for a Legendary status. Now, we will start anew. Today, you take back your territory.

Pro tip: perception has an unrecognized influence.

Perception is the dividing line that separates reality from that which is incomprehensible. So, learning to have a flexible perception is one of the most valuable lessons a person can undergo. Ultimately,we treat things according to the uses we ascribe to them and, oftentimes, we fail to consider the actual potential they hold. Sometimes, the entire process of ascribing purpose and value can work against you because of a failure to be mindful of the power of perception.

So, let's change our perspective on territory.

Start by taking the 3,000 named accounts that have been put in your hopper, which we discussed last week, and dwindle them down to 300 or approximately 10%. Why? Two reasons:

First, because less is more. Recognize that your territory is where you eat, sleep, breath, struggle, and succeed. It can build you up or tear you down... all based on the way you view it and the care with which you treat it. So. having a smaller list allows you to be more intentional with each prospect and will give you a much different level of success inside your territory.

Secondly, because you don't have 50 years to spare. Especially while only making a small portion of the available commissions that are staring back at you wondering if you'll ever recognize their existence.

So, let's look at a new way to plan out and execute engaging our territory. We'll start by choosing 25 accounts from your curated list. Now, it's time to truly engage them, no generic phone call, no quick stop-in to "leave some information" in hopes they'll call. No, we are moving to intentional actions that will cause a ripple effect throughout each organization you interact and engage with.

Take a moment to think about your first date. Did you walk in without smelling your absolute best, wearing your fanciest shirt, or sporting those fitted pants to accentuate your "you know what!" You looked, smelled, and were, your absolute best. Everything coming out of your mouth was carefully thought out and articulated in an intentional manner. Maybe you were a bit vulnerable, maybe you showed empathy in your conversation. Either way, you were the real you and listened intently, asking thoughtful questions with genuine care... why should prospecting be any different? All too often we forget that interaction with other human-beings is sacred, and not a game.

Quickly go through each business on your list of 25. Get on LinkedIn, get on Twitter, check out Facebook for Business, find everything you can about your prospect as a whole by utilizing the tools which are literally at your fingertips. This is a concerted effort toward making sure each of the 25 prospects on your horizon will meet with you. Once you have a feel for the account and the folks who reside within, grab your FTPs and head into the field.

So, let's do the math on this equation (using the formula from Day 2) to better understand the end result we're seeking. We're curating 25 accounts per day with intentionality using interrupt marketing in order to have a conversation with all 25 accounts.

Let's say 15 of these conversations with these accounts gain you traction and you end up with 7 immediate appointments. Let's say those appointments turn into 2.5 total closes per week. At $7.5k per deal, you are closing almost $20k weekly from this daily workflow of curated accounts. Plus, you're going all-in on your prospecting efforts using the R.E.A.S.O.N. theory.

Do that consistently and you've got yourself $80k in closable business per month. "BS!" is what you're saying right now. Go ahead, prove us wrong. It's guaranteed you will, but not in the way you think... soome of you will prospect 25 targeted accounts like a true Rebel, get 24 appointments, and close 20 deals in the course of 3 months. Some of you will only get 7 appointments, complain about it, and fail to realize that 7 is still 5 more than you're use to having!

This is the method of the Rebellion! The method that will set you apart from the infinite indistinguishability and cause a tidal wave of success... if you choose to hone into the principles we are laying before you.

We're not saying that if you start this week these are the numbers you will obtain. This is a methodized process which will have a snowball effect over time. The amount of time is relative to your ability to be enthusiastic about your R.E.A.S.O.N. and what kind of buying cycle your market falls under.

It's important to understand that all verticals have a different sales cycle and that your professional career in sales is a long journey. There's no short term relief, no immediate reward. If you thought differently before, then, you've just been taken to church. Accept the truth and welcome your new sales reality.

Allow this new method of prospecting in your territory to bother you. If you feel you don't agree, great. That's your perception kicking in. The old school mentality of "you have to make a million calls on the phone, period." We're working with you to kick that habit. Remember the second paragraph of this day? Go back and read it as a quick reminder...

We'll tell you again, this method takes time and a willingness to invest in yourself, however, it's the game changer you've been seeking. Every time you've sat at your desk on a payday wondering how you can put more commission into your check is coming to fruition at this very moment. These are the approaches The Copier Warrior used to build his castle, and now... they're yours.

What will you build with them?

TAKE A FEW MOMENTS AND REFLECT ON THE QUOTE AT THE BEGINNING OF THE DAY...

TODAY'S ADVENTURE

Select the 300 accounts out of your territory. Make this number relevant to your vertical. For example, If you only have 100 people you're seeking to serve, take 10-15 (as long as it won't get you fired) and engage them using your R.E.A.S.O.N. theory.

_____
_____
_____
_____
_____
_____
_____
_____
_____
_____
_____
_____
_____
_____
_____
_____
_____
_____
_____
_____
_____
_____
_____
_____

THE WARRIOR'S WORDS:

To give you a real-time scenario on why it is important to dive into your prospect's social channels when learning more about them... all territories have a digital aspect to them now....

There once was an account in Orlando that had tweeted out their frustration about the copier they were using. I used the post to create a very fun and entertaining FTP that would speak to their issue with the equipment. They bought from me just a few months later and canceled their contract with the incumbent. The best part? The one you would think was the decision maker, due to the vertical and nature of their business, wasn't the "decision maker" at all... I was also able to identify this through their social channels. Boom and boom.

In the copier industry, a prospect usually has a 3–5 year commitment on their office equipment. So if you walk in 2 weeks after they just signed a 3-year deal, you're going to have to put the prospect into your Living Pipeline as they won't be doing anything for quite some time. In this particular instance, prospecting efforts utilizing our R.E.A.S.O.N. theory will cause the customer to feel a bit of regret that they didn't know you existed before they made their decision. This gives you plenty of time to utilize your Chest of Wonder to nurture the relationship you've started building.

DAY 10

THE WANDERER'S BACKPACK

--- NAPOLEON BONAPARTE ---

"The human race is governed by its imagination."

This week's prospecting lesson is brought to you by the one and only: "Wanderer's Backpack."

Prospecting is more than just a part of your role. Prospecting is the very fiber of a successful salesperson. This goes back to every day leading up to this lesson — your habits, service to your community, your Roots, and understanding your territory from a fresh new perspective. These subjects are important to keep top of mind as you develop your backpack and your wandering skills.

Today we're going to give you a peek into the Sales Rebellion's backpack. Let's start with LinkedIn, every salesperson's best friend. Go ahead, pull up one of the 25 organizations on your list for today.

Here are some of the things to look out for and to do:
- Read about when the company was founded
- Read their bio describing "who they are"
- Check out any website links they have on their page
- Scroll through to find all the relevant information needed
- Check out their content feed and see what they're talking about on an ongoing basis
- Get to know them from a high-level perspective
- Click follow and keep them in your personal feed
- Click on "See all 343 employees" and get the magic started
- Look for the key contact that holds the position or title you would be connecting with
- Take a look at their personal profile to better understand the personality of the buyer

Now, when going through the employee list, remember that their title is not as important as you might think... the objective is to find the key decision makers of the organization. Don't forget, most businesses keep a very well updated business page on both LinkedIn and Facebook. Plus, they're normally speaking directly to their buying audience.

When we say "understand the personality of the buyer," we don't mean, "They went to UCF and are endorsed by 56 people for 'strategic planning'." We're talking about understanding their personality, their likes and dislikes as an individual — They are so much more than "they went to UCF to major in blah blah yadda yadda." Always be looking for what makes them "tick" look for their *WHY*. Hopefully, they have put hints of this in their bio. If the individual posts or interacts with others on LinkedIn, you'll be able to see it. This will help you better understand how they think and what they're passionate about.

Remember, you might be surprised by what you typically find in their feed. You'll learn that ... they're actual people... with opinions... who are engaging... Not a CB-1-2-MANY — *queue robot voice* — "Who will not take a meeting with you." It **is** okay to send them a connection request, but please, for the love of all that is Holy, do not "connect and pitch"... Instead, be a pattern interrupt in their daily habits and activities.

Try a message like this:

> *"Thanks for connecting! Looking forward to engaging with you and your business through content. And, if there is ever anything I can do in order to ease the pain when using *insert your product here* just summon me. I respond quickest to the sound of a conch shell in the pitch of E major. Excited to know you better!"*
> *-Your Name*

Remember, this is a first touch. Not everyone is going to write you back and tell you to come sell them something — that's not the focus anyway. This is the first part of a tailored process to get deeper with your prospect, to truly cause meaningful and genuine connection. It's much different than the traditional "dial and dump" or "knock and barf" process that the sales world traditionally teaches.

When done correctly, the difference people are looking for is exemplified in your first interaction. Don't be afraid of the unknown. Without guts, there can be no glory. What's the worst that could happen? They don't accept your request? What happens to you currently during those 100 dials you make? Do people hang up? Tell you they're"not interested!"? Tell you they're "all set!"? Tell you "no thanks"? You already get rejected on a daily basis, why wouldn't you take a chance on yourself and the idea of becoming a Legend inside of your sales community?

Building credibility through your tailored first touch and by being more relevant to the generation you're selling to? Adapt or die, Sales Legends.

History was not made by people who were afraid of change. It was made by people who envisioned the future and sought out ways to make it a reality.

Recognize the Rebellion that is taking place:

Everyone wants a more humanizing experience in the sales world. Yet, the features and benefits of commodity selling are usually the first things out of sales peoples' mouths. Stop wasting your time with tactics of the past and start personifying what the future will be made of... Authenticity

TAKE A FEW MOMENTS AND REFLECT ON THE QUOTE AT THE BEGINNING OF THE DAY...

TODAY'S ADVENTURE

Start engaging your list of prospects on LinkedIn, make 25 new connections today. Start developing a pattern interrupt marketing piece specifically designed for these prospects as you begin to better understand them through research. In other words, start building your backpack.

THE WARRIOR'S WORDS:

You should not be mindlessly scrolling through the internet, looking for information on your customer. This should be focused, intentional learning about the prospect and their affiliations. This should also not take very long for you to do. Go back to Day 8 and see the bullet point on the daily routine where we talk about doing research on your curated 25 for the day. Once you get good at this, you can start getting ahead of yourself and have your research done a week in advance.

If you use a note in your connection request on LinkedIn, do not be misleading with the note and say: "I wanted to add you to my professional network as it seems we have a lot in common." This message makes me want to vomit. Instead, send them something like this: "Well hello. My name's Dale Dupree, but my friends call me The Copier Warrior. I wanted to connect as it seems that you would definitely be a great asset when the Zombie Apocalypse hits earth. In turn, when copiers/printers have learned our weaknesses and attempt to rule over mankind, I promise to protect you."

DAY 11

ALLIANCES... THE REAL GOAL OF NETWORKING

DALE CARNEGIE

> "You can make more friends in two months by becoming interested in other people than you can in two years trying to get other people interested in you."

Now is a good time to reflect on the attitude discussed in prior days. Remember the statement made around referral relationships/networking? Good, now let's talk more about the Rebellion's methods behind Alliances. There's nothing quite like being introduced to someone that has a need for your services by someone they trust. It's not a sure win, but if you can connect with the referral the same way you did with your client, it can bear some pretty tasty fruit.

Networking can be pretty intense. One thing to keep top of mind when focused on developing your networking skills is that most people do it wrong. When you show up to the local meet-up group and look around, what do you see? A bunch of salespeople passing cards to each other trying to sell everyone in the room their services? Yeah, probably.

Instead, every salesperson needs to be looking at these types of events as an opportunity to align themselves with folks in the community. The same ones that are out hunting for, and developing businesses of their own, who can become power players, and take your networking game to another level.

Understand also, you need to be a Rebel to those who network with you as well. It's why attitude is so important in sales. If you're focused on true service, you'll be a deep well full of business opportunities for other sales folks in your network. Why? Because your customers will come to you for help in finding vendors/services that their businesses need. You've not only earned credibility, but they'll also see you as a champion of the community, and trust your circles run deep. This is something that's developed over time through focus and patience. So, how do you start networking? Here are a few simple ideas...

- Get with your best customers and see if they're in networking groups of their own — ask if you can come as a visitor
- Get online and search for local networking groups. Scroll through and try to find ones that are relevant to you
- Some meetup groups will be tailored toward specific industries and don't invite random vendors to their events. (Make a note: these are some of the absolute best to attend. They just take time to get into in most cases.)
- What? You said you are an SDR/BDR? No worries. Host a "virtual lunch" with colleagues and clients to introduce one another in order to expand their businesses. You'll be rewarded for this type of effort. Also, make sure you ask each guest you invite to think of other members that could be added to the group
- If you are a millennial, look for groups that are titled as "Young Professional Group" or "YPG" for short

Go out and shake people's hands, ask them what they do so you can understand whether or not you can help. Also, consider who might be talking to prospects you would like to cultivate into clients. Don't be short-sighted. You don't know who these people know. A good relationship with them could open many different doors.

Collect everyone's cards and, when doing so, make a small mental note about a detail you discussed with that person. It takes some practice, but correlating the detail with something on the card helps — or just write on the card if you're really that bad at remembering things. Then, take some time the following day to write a thank you note with your business card inside so if they ever need to reach out to you, they now have it.

Mention the small detail that you remembered from the conversation. This will cause them to view you differently because it's a sacrifice of your time to sit and write out thoughtful thank you notes to folks you just met. It's part of your new service above self attitude — your goal in doing this is to earn their trust, and trust is earned through credibility. People have to believe you are what you say. You don't just have to earn the decision maker's trust, you have to earn everyone's trust.

Remember that networking is focused on people helping people meet folks they otherwise would have struggled to connect with. This action is reciprocated by them as well. However, when you're investing your word in someone via a referral, make sure they are worthy of you risking your own reputation. The idea behind this is that you're sacrificing your time to flirt with destiny, a better way to work and a more satisfying version of success.

Don't take networking lightly. Put your heart and soul into it and remember some of the key tips we have given you today. The key is to approach networking with a giving mindset, not a taking mindset. Give at every opportunity without expectation of reciprocity and see what happens in time.

TAKE A FEW MOMENTS AND REFLECT ON THE QUOTE AT THE BEGINNING OF THE DAY...

TODAY'S ADVENTURE

Create a list of local networking groups and divide them into three categories: group size, meeting location, commitments/requirements. Then, join at least one, commit time, and give everything you got to those you meet and engage with!

_____

_____

_____

_____

_____

_____

_____

_____

_____

_____

_____

_____

_____

THE WARRIOR'S WORDS:

Networking was the cornerstone of my sales success. Sometimes, I found my best referral sources from dropping off a coffee-stained letter, or a not-so-business card that interrupted the normal patterns a prospect was use to receiving. By taking these extra steps to give people a better sales experience, we slowly earn their trust over time. Trust is what leads to your name being spoken outside of a problem with the widget or service you sell. Trust builds more than just loyal clients, it produces raving fans of, and for, your personal brand. People willing to go out of their own way to see that you are rewarded. If you want to receive this kind of attention... give it, earn it, and build a culture around it.

DAY 12 K.N.O.W.

OLIVER WENDELL HOLMES

"It is the province of knowledge to speak, and it is the privilege of wisdom to listen."

We've discussed the true knowledge that Rebels need to be focused on while seeking to understand more than just whether or not your product is being USED inside of a business. This only scrapes the surface and cuts you off short. Here, we'll talk about how to sharpen our knowledge of a prospect/decision maker without becoming their own personal sales stalker.

This is one of the hardest processes to develop, but once a groove is established, you will become unstoppable. This day is about being in the K.N.O.W. about everything and anything that a local business/community has going on. This is a huge part of the education process when working toward a healthy first touch/appointment and ongoing relationship with each of your potential prospects. Stay patient in this process, keep diligent, and be prepared to embrace the suck — this is not easy.

Let's talk about verticals in regards to K.N.O.W.

There's a huge difference between a medical firm and a manufacturer (unless you're selling a vertical-specific product). Odds are, these two industries will have different uses for the widget you're selling. The principle use might be the same (for example, they each utilize the printer you sell) but the end result and workflows will vary due to their industry-specific deliverables. So, how do we educate ourselves on their processes without having a meeting first? With one of the many tools in The Wanderer's Backpack.

When it comes to the manufacturer, a great way to gain more knowledge of their business is to engage with their operation through a public tour of their facility. For example, there are several boat manufacturers in Florida that give public tours once or twice a month that ANYONE can sign up for. They walk you through the entire facility and, in most cases, they tell you EVERYTHING about the operation and sometimes introduce you to individual department heads.

The important part to remember here? You will become educated on *HOW* their business makes money. All the processes in which they accomplish this, who they serve, who they're connected with, how their employees operate inside their business, etc. This will allow you to understand how your product or service offering will complement their internal workflow.

This method of educating yourself on the customer takes you to the heart of how they create their widget or service. This is a piece of the puzzle. How can you help them with these processes through your products/services? Will this stabilize or enhance their economic outcomes?

Now, let's jump over to the medical vertical for a second because you're saying to yourself, "they don't give tours at a family practice in Saginaw, Michigan." And you're right, you will have to think further outside the box. People usually suggest "researching the vertical," but that doesn't help much as you are just filling your brain with generic information.

Cool, you know what a Dinglehopper and a Snarfblat are — no one else cares. Instead, head toward local resources like the newspaper or a national magazine that has honored a specific doctor at the firm. In this approach, it's more about understanding and appreciating someone or something about an individual or the business.

To maximize the effectiveness of this strategy, you need to find information that speaks to the culture of the firm. Maybe they've innovated a new process at their firm that is used globally. Maybe, it's a local impact they've had on the community through volunteer work. Or, perhaps they give 3 months paid maternity leave, or do something specific for their employees that most businesses don't.

Additionally, you can find out which charities they're involved in. A local project such as a little league baseball team, their involvement with The Boys and Girls Club, etc. Most will have a writeup on the individual or business itself, his/her or the company's accomplishments, how their firm is growing and innovating in the community, and so on.

The point of these methods is to gain a next-level understanding of the *WHY* of the firm and also exactly what topics are most important to them... which is one piece of how you will relate your product or service as a solution.

It's important to know that sincerity is the key ingredient in this method and there is a very fine line to walk. Thus, we're not using this information to get a "YES" decision on a transaction. Rather, we're using it to strengthen the business relationship with our prospect. Your intention is as equally important as your action.

Next, let's talk about the internet tools in the Wanderer's Backpack. We've talked about prospecting and targeting through social mediums, which can be applied toward educating yourself on the buyer and his/her firm. For example, you can check their content feeds or read any articles they're sharing/participating in. But let's talk about the next pieces of the puzzle... Google Alerts, The Local Newspaper, and the EDC.

Go to google.com/alerts, type in keywords like "business expansion in (insert) County" and Google will send you an email alert anytime a local or national media entity uses the keywords that you've entered. The email will link you back to articles, interviews, and information that is key to understanding more about the businesses in your local marketplace from a fact-gathering standpoint. This will also serve as a unique tool that will help build the foundation of your interactions with the prospect.

One local media entity the millennial generation has lost touch with is... the newspaper. To some of us, it was that thing that one of our wealthy uncles paid $400 a year to be delivered every Sunday. For others, we flashback to Paperboy on Super Nintendo and recall how proud we are of our high score that none of our friends could ever beat! But, we digress... the point is that we've lost touch with such a medium because technology has placed the news at our fingertips in real-time. But it should be known that there is a lot of activity in the local paper that never makes it onto televised news. And the best thing about the newspaper is that it's a consolidated information database of current events across a local region. Ultimately, it can pay off big to know what's happening in your Uncle's dusty old newspaper.

Another local entity for your Wanderer's Backpack is the local Economic Development Commission (EDC). Your EDC is a powerhouse for business growth in the community. They have great relationships with existing businesses that are expanding, and they know all about the players that are coming to town in the near future. Not only do they have knowledge of growth/expansion, but they often put on educational workshops, and do quarterly meetings/updates regarding the state of the County/City/State at which everyone and their mum show up to listen.

This allows you to shake hands with the movers and shakers of the community and to gain more education on the firms in your community through discussions and presentations.

Adapting and evolving to an attitude of service allows you to understand fully what this subject is all about. It's not about you, it's about them. How can you truly care about the businesses you're serving if you don't K.N.O.W. who they really are and how they support the individuals that work there? How can you truly know how they bless the local charities that impact and change the very fiber of their beloved community? You need to see the bigger picture if you're ever going to #ChangeTheGame for yourself, your sales career, and those you serve.

Whether you take a tour, link up with the EDC, or subscribe to Google Alerts, the focus here is to be a Rebel by asking questions — learn, listen, and interact. Dive into what's important to the businesses around you, what makes them tick, why they are in your area in the first place, what they take pride in, what their culture consists of... Go deeper!

Ultimately, the world is a system of systems. The more you know about how they operate, the better you'll be able to connect the right pieces... with the right places.

TAKE A FEW MOMENTS AND REFLECT ON THE QUOTE AT THE BEGINNING OF THE DAY...

TODAY'S ADVENTURE

Explore the tools above, subscribe to Google Alerts, and begin getting acquainted with your local EDC.

THE WARRIOR'S WORDS:

Get to know the individual journalists who are reporting on the business community. They're a dynamic resource that can open different doors for you. They'll provide you with unique information and perspectives on the happenings in your backyard and, in most cases, can give you direct introductions to the businesses you want to meet.

Let's face it, it's not just the newspaper people have disconnected with, it's all local media publications. It is a shame because the local media outlets are valuable resources to a sales career... if properly utilized. I am loyal to them. Here's an example: there was an article in a local Brevard County media outlet that gave me a short history of the founding and expansion of a local firm. There were tons of details on them in this article — a goldmine of information! I then used it to help craft my first touch with one of the individuals at their business who had been featured. They eventually introduced me to the decision maker and became my client.

DAY 13
REFLECTIVE CONNECTIONS

PROVERBS 27:3

"As a man thinketh in his heart, so is he."

One thing asked of every Rebel is that you dig deep and go beyond the surface level of sales tactics. You've experienced a lot of this culture so far: personal and professional habits, expanding perspective on your territory and prospecting, purpose, service, community, attitudes, and so much more. It can be a lot to take in, especially if you're new to the sales world or heavily grounded in a different sales belief system. That's why it's important to understand that giving time to process these teachings is critical to your success.

To steal a line from Dr. Richard Bommelje, "Reflection is the learning after the learning." Reflect on everything you've experienced thus far: the readings in the book, your interactions with people, leadership at work, and yourself within all of it. It's in this reflection that puzzle pieces connect and changes can and will take place.

Reflection is about more than just "me." It's a way for you to be held accountable to the impact you're making on others which, if done mindfully, will better those around you as well. Think of reflection as a powerful tool to help you attain the next level you're looking for in sales, and to help you make the Rebellious impact on others that they long to experience.

Change, though inconvenient, is inevitable.

TAKE A FEW MOMENTS AND REFLECT ON THE QUOTE AT THE BEGINNING OF THE DAY...

TODAY'S ADVENTURE

Reflect and reconnect with your true self.

DAY 14 SELF-LESS

THEODORE ROOSEVELT

"...if you are too timid or too fastidious or too careless to do your part in this work, then you forfeit your right to be considered one of the governing and you become the governed instead..."

Service is life.

In order to develop a more intimate relationship with your community, you must put some skin in the game and give back. But what's most important about giving, is not the money or material items, it's the motivation behind it. You can give money in austerity under real hope that it is helpful. You can also give money in a manipulative manner with the expectation of receiving something for it. It's the difference between putting other people before yourself and taking action based solely on a "what's in it for me" attitude.

PRO TIP:
Next level success is directly connected
to next level responsibility.

It takes courage to help others and it takes wisdom to know what they truly need. Some people really do just need money to get back on their feet. For others, money is the last thing they need. Thus, learning to recognize and read the moment is one of the most valuable skills a person can develop. However, it's not enough to just know what the moment needs. It also takes the courage to act on those realizations.

So, how do we apply this attitude of service at work? Have you ever considered why the receptionist was so "rude" to you? What if you learned that their family member was diagnosed with a terminal illness earlier that morning? Or, their father passed away recently and today was especially difficult... Or that it just sucks at their office due to the toxic culture and a boss who clearly needs some Jesus in his life. What if you wore this attitude of service on your sleeve during your first interactions with this individual? You might just shine much-needed light into the person's life you're interacting with. Life doesn't pause between 8:00 am and 5:00 pm.

Take pride in your ability to be able to give back... not everyone wakes up in a bed, inside a house, with a fridge full of food. Have you ever experienced losing everything? If you were in that situation, would you appreciate someone offering an olive branch? We are not saying to give everything you have away; we're saying start looking at what you have to give — this has the most impact.

Sales starts with service.

TAKE A FEW MOMENTS AND REFLECT ON THE QUOTE AT THE BEGINNING OF THE DAY...

TODAY'S ADVENTURE

Did you give something away last week? If not, today is a new day. If so, kudos! Write it down and describe your experience. Today is another opportunity to give back to your community, family, friends, and loved ones. Give something away today without the expectation of reciprocity... Again.

DAY 15
PURPOSEFUL PROSPECTING AND AN EMPTY STOMACH

> ## PABLO PICASSO
> *"To draw, you must close your eyes and sing."*

Between 8:00 am and 12:00 pm, your #1 goal is to be out interacting with your community. The proper sales term for this would be a form of "cold calling." Just grab your curated list, snatch up your FTPs, get in the car, and head into the community because, for the next several hours, you'll be focused on making impactful first impressions.

As you're out canvassing, remember to be confident in your ability and desire to serve your community. When you pull into their parking lot, feel confident. Remember everything we've learned from The Copier Warrior in prior days leading up to this moment.

Some of you have heard of the infamous Crumpled Letter... well, this is the part of the day where we drop those off. This is one of many FTPs we suggest Rebels use. To learn more head over to www.crumpledletter.com. You'll spend the next several hours making meaningful in-person calls with intentionality and having a blast doing so! Some folks will see your FTPs come across their desk and ring you straight away before you can get out of the parking lot! Others will call and set an appointment without you having to call them back. But remember that all the people you've encountered will become an individual/company whom you'll be dialing, and quite possibly connecting with later.

This will absolutely fill your time for the next 3+ hours. Once you get your desired number of drops, remember to check your email/phone. Respond to calls, texts, emails, inbound through social media — as you will need to focus on "staying in the loop" while you are out building your future.

Now, it's time for lunch!

The Copier Warrior lived by a very important rule, never eat by yourself. Make sure that you're taking a client, prospect, friend or even family member to lunch with you every day. It's important to use this time as a relaxation moment in the day, and to do so with an attitude of thankfulness, and an understanding that people thrive on human interaction.You're taking someone with you so that you can learn about them them on a deeper level, so you can connect with them human to human. When it comes to your prospects/clients, these are the types of interactions which cause a referral relationship to organically blossom and will keep clients coming back year over year.

Now, we all know you're not always going to have a lunch partner planned out. So, here's some Sales Rebellion secret sauce on the subject: when you don't have someone lined up for lunch, head to one of the local restaurants that have a "community table" where anybody and everybody can sit together. Find a few folks that are already in fellowship and ask permission to sit and chat with them. If you're feeling weird about it, make it weirder and tell them this:

> *"Hey, this crazy, absurdly ridiculous book that I'm reading has a rule that I'm not supposed to eat lunch alone. I wasn't able to get any of my clients or friends away from work for lunch today, so I wanted to ask if it was okay that I joined you in fellowship while we all ate. It would be an honor, and I'll put all the waters on my bill."*

It's important you understand we're not telling you that you have to pay for lunch every day. If you're on a budget, or you prefer to pack your lunch, brilliant — Setup a "virtual" lunch with your prospect or client instead. Or, grab a co-worker in the office and get to know them better. No excuses! Don't eat lunch alone!

Maybe you're not into the community table... that's cool... there are ample opportunities to connect with others via technology as well. It's definitely not hard to pull out the phone and have some FaceTime with your spouse or loved one. There are also groups who meet for lunch via Zoom in a networking and community building fashion. The point is, people are out there, and it benefits you greatly to use lunch as an opportunity to connect with other human beings.

WELCOME TO THE NEXT LEVEL.

It's not easy to get this part of your day well oiled and working as the machine it's meant to be. Remember, a lot of what you're doing in this section takes guts, and forever remember — no guts no glory. Let's not forget to stay focused on what the overall picture of the day is. You're making meaningful touches, whether it is during your first call, or over the best tacos in your local community with a total stranger. You're stepping out on a limb by doing uncomfortable things that lead you into engaging individuals you, otherwise, would have never met. It's a leap of faith — a promise to yourself that you will live a meaningful life.

TAKE A FEW MOMENTS AND REFLECT ON THE QUOTE AT THE BEGINNING OF THE DAY...

TODAY'S ADVENTURE

Get lunch with complete strangers.

THE WARRIOR'S WORDS:

Do not allow your mind to wander during the day. If you don'tstay in the loop... your hard work will cause you to sink deep into the swamp of self-defeat. What I'm saying is, time management is so important that if you don't keep track of it *you will* be on the losing side of the equation.

I have an entire mindset and experience related to your role in breaking through to each account as you stop in and leave your FTPs. Engage the receptionist, build rapport — don't just leave the touch piece and walk out. Create an *experience* for the folks you're calling on. Go ahead, ask to see the decision maker... hand them the letter yourself! If you just drop and go, you'll most likely lose momentum on the marketing piece you have carefully crafted. Be inquisitive with everyone you speak with, allow the storytelling methodology to naturally take effect through every conversation. This will help to get the brain firing on all cylinders, cause walls to crumble, and set the narrative for a successful sales call.

Remember, the idea is to be something completely different than EVERY.OTHER.SALESPERSON. that walks through their front door. You also have to be focused on creating a result for yourself — a connection, a laugh — NOT A SALE. This first interaction is not about anything other than introducing yourself (not your product), learning more about who they are, and learning more about what they do. It's not about how your product can increase productivity.

Don't hear me wrong here. The sale will come naturally as you walk with them down this road less traveled by the sales community. This is the true secret sauce you're looking for... If they love the marketing piece, but they're not interested in your product (at this time), then the last thing you should be focused on is setting an appointment — they won't want one! Instead, think about the long term with these encounters:

- How do you naturally build a relationship with another human being?
- How do you apply that to the business friendship you're looking to develop with this firm you are calling on?

Gotcha thinking, don't I?

True value is not just based on the product, your knowledge, or the appointment to present your services. True value is something earned... over time... with credibility and hard work. It's based around the principles of basic human interaction and the psychology behind why one person will buy from another. Initial interactions are the *keys* to this type of success.

Some people will read your Crumpled Letter/Coffee Stained Letter*... whatever touch piece you're dropping off and instantly ask you to quote them. You have to practice the same mentality with them as well... *BUILD THE RELATIONSHIP!* Let them naturally buy. If they're ready to rock 'n roll in this moment, stay focused on the long term outlook just the same as the people who are "not interested at this time." The overall message here? Be different, be authentic, treat your prospects respectfully and with the intention of serving them for the rest of your existence as a sales professional. Don't be a one sale wonder. Want to learn more? Jump over to *www.salesrebellion.com* and join the Rebellion like all the other individual contributors before you. These Rebels have Chosen Legendary and want to better understand how to sharpen these types of interactions.

> *Don't forget, to learn more about our most popular FTP that interrupts the typical patterns and is setting appointments and closing deals for sellers all over the world... www.crumpledletter.com*

DAY 18

TERRITORY PART 3 — THE NEXT LEVEL

ALBERT EINSTEIN

"A hundred times a day I remind myself that my inner and outer life are based on the labors of other men, living and dead, and that I must exert myself in order to give in the same measure as I have received and am still receiving."

Think deep.

Consider one of the businesses on the top of your curated list. This business was created by a person or group of people. It exists because individuals choose to work there. Folks answer the phones, send emails, process orders, file requisition forms, and everything else that it takes to operate a business. But then... most of them go home and live totally unrelated lives. They run marathons, struggle with addiction, adopt children, fight cancer, collect exotic butterflies, play Dungeons & Dragons, volunteer at homeless shelters, and bury their loved ones during seasons of loss. This list is endless. But it's important to know that these are the unspoken threads that weave us all together.

When we realize we're connected to our territory in ways we never imagined, we begin to realize the value of the impact we can have. People don't consciously know it, but they want to have their personal and professional lives meld. They want community, service, and purpose. But we're conditioned by society, that these things are oil and water. That to make boatloads of money, one has to operate within a high degree of selfishness, or that to really make an impact one must give up material goods.

This is why changing your perspective on territory is so important. We can single-handedly have a meaningful outcome with every person in our community, and not sacrifice our own success by simply changing the way we approach it.

Know now that a far-reaching impact on your territory will come from your "Living Pipeline" and the work you put into it. Understand that you should work to develop a symbiotic relationship with your territory. Realize that you must take ownership in the fact that you share your territory with a community of individuals — people from your office that work alongside you — folks in charge of finances at the local manufacturing firm — people who develop their own products and services — those who are economically sound and those who struggle to make a buck. They're all living members of your Living Pipeline.

What is a "Living Pipeline" you ask? To fully understand, you have to know that your sales funnel has always been about numbers. That your efforts have previously been focused on a massive amount of prospecting activity, and because of this... you make 100 calls to get anything and everything packed into your funnel, only to turn around and do it again tomorrow.

As Rebels, we also usually think of the funnel as holding a 30/60/90/120 day list of prospects inside of it.

However, a Living Pipeline is populated with many different fruits. Whether it's someone four weeks out from buying or four years away from taking bids; every single person/business that you meet, who has a need for your services, or knows someone in need of your services... should be the apple of your eye, regardless of whether or not they are buying right this second. They are all alive in your Living Pipeline.

Think of your Living Pipeline as a tree; roots deep into the soil, branches both weathered and refined. Each branch symbolizes a different section of your Living Pipeline. At the bottom of the tree, we have our Roots, the foundation of your sales processes.

At the trunk of the tree lies your Chest of Wonder and the process of breaking through the noise in order to find qualified prospects. The branches are defined by prospect classification and time.

Prospect Classification Branches:

Whales, Walruses, Wild Cards and Not Interested — segment the prospect by key factors and place them into the appropriate branch. Each branch has a specified communication strategy designed to build relationships and identify where the sales process is at.

Time and Type Related Branches:

3/6/9/120, 12 Month, Two Years Plus, GrandDADs — all place a prospect onto a specific branch according to the time remaining until a client is taking bids or renewing their agreement. Not Interested, Wild Cards and Whales & Walruses all represent a different type of buyer or business that need a more robust system of experiential interactions. Each branch has a communication cadence designed to ensure that you have a better chance of securing the relationship, and winning the sale.

Here's a brief explanation of each branch:

- 30/60/90/120 days - these folks are all making decisions within a week to 4 months and will have a different focus than most sales you find as the timeframe is short and they need to be cultivated with a unique attitude all the way to the finish line. Here is an example workflow for a buyer who resides in this branch:
- 12 months - these folks have enough time remaining that you can explore a nurturing approach — you have time to break down barriers and earn credibility through your marketing efforts and different types/styles of interactions. But be ready, they could make changes at any point now. Don't think that everyone will wait until the lease date expires on their contracts.

- 2 years - these are the people with whom you are engaging with on a whole other level! — you're keeping them abreast of your latest content, building credibility through unique touches, next level encounters, watering your branch, and helping it to bear fruit. Here is an example workflow for a buyer that you have found who resides in branch:
- **GrandDADs** - these are the folks who are WAAAAAY out from making any kind of decision on your products and services. You're focused on keeping a more intimate relationship with them by staying in touch over holidays, through special occasions, romanticizing your future business relationship... as you graduate them into the lower branches.
- **Not Interested!** - these are the folks who have rejected your approach and put you in the "sales box." They use your products and services currently with another provider, so you know they're a legitimate prospect, but they are "happy" where they are at and have not given you anything else to work with. We have a branch for these, they are not dead until the fat lady sings.... thrice...
- **Wild Cards** - these are the folks where anything can happen. Maybe they don't re-evaluate their current situation for 4 years, but they are so unhappy with the product that they could pull the trigger to make a change at any minute. Or, they could wait 4 years... you just don't know.
- **Whales and Walruses** - these are what you would qualify as a BIG account, major account, global account, whatever the heck your flavor is for an account bigger than down-the-street business. We have an entire playbook for courting these types of clients. They require a much different approach in order to differentiate yourself from the competition and cause an awakening that leads to a sale.

It's important to cultivate a Living Pipeline. This is a new approach to the way we interact and develop a deeper relationship with the businesses we aim to serve. No more "Just Checking-In" emails. No more voicemail after voicemail being left. Instead, take an active approach — one that changes the game for the prospect. Be mindful that it's easy for these branches to grow old and die, mainly out of neglect. Thus, diligence and time management are key components to keeping your tree young and spry, flourishing with fruit.

Be intentional with your prospects and they will reward you with their trust.

TAKE A FEW MOMENTS AND REFLECT ON THE QUOTE AT THE BEGINNING OF THE DAY...

TODAY'S ADVENTURE

Begin creating your Living Pipeline. Who's on your 2-year branch? Who's on your 12-month branch? Who are your wildcards? Is your tree full of fruit... or is your pipeline rusty and leaking?

_____

_____

_____

_____

_____

_____

_____

_____

_____

_____

_____

_____

_____

THE WARRIOR'S WORDS:

There is so much more substance to the concepts above. Head on over to www.salesrebellion.com in order to better understand how to properly cultivate a Living Pipeline.

*Please also note that workflow(s) is/are based on a cold call that turned into an opportunity to sell your product/service — this means there could be a decision within 2-3 weeks or 4 years from your first touch. There are massive amounts of little details being left out. If we put it all in there your head might explode. *

DAY 17

A CHEST FULL OF WONDER

— ALFRED NORTH WHITEHEAD —

"We cannot think first and act afterwards. From the moment of birth we are immersed in action, and can only fitfully guide it by taking thought."

"Make 100 calls because you have to," at least in order to get an appointment... Right?

Wrong. This is action without thought. Today we address the Chest of Wonder in which all mediums reside. The contents within will help you to build the foundation of your relationships with each and every prospect. These mediums are not your business cards and tri-fold brochures the firm gave you to hand out. Things within your Chest of Wonder interrupt the normal patterns of our buyers and cause undeniable curiosity which gives the prospect an awakening.

Your Chest of Wonder should be plentiful. You should have a tool for each stage inside your sales process. For example, once you have met with a prospect and they've agreed to take the next step with you by demoing your product and receiving a proposal, you should be armed with personalized handwritten notes you send to the prospect in order to take them deeper into the process you're building with them. It's not just a thank you card — it has expanded knowledge attached to it, more about your R.E.A.S.O.N. that your prospect has yet to uncover, and is a gesture of kindness and respect.

There are four parts to your Chest of Wonder:

- **Your Brand** - Dale Dupree was, and always will be, "The Copier Warrior." Use www.copierwarrior.com to see his presence and to understand what we mean by "Your Brand." You've built the foundation, now put up the walls. Be unapologetically authentic, be human, be you!
- **Your Content** - This is the awareness behind your brand. Here, you'll utilize marketing collateral to build on your messaging. Salespeople of the future build credibility on a deeper level with their prospects and clients. To do that, start creating copy/content that moves mountains.
- **Your Xochil Presence** - This is your overall presence online and within social media platforms. The value and importance of this cannot be overstated. This is the catalyst for community building and an integral part of your Living Pipeline.
- **The Awakening** - This represents your First Touch Pieces (FTPs) such as our Rebel Letter Campaign, The Rebel Resume, The Unwritten Story, The Empty Donut Box, or our Not-So-Business-Card; as well as follow-up marketing materials, interactive experiences for people that are ghosting you, and even tools to help with your closing stages. The main goal is to give your prospect a unique experience and keep them engaged.

These methods are intended to feel like a treasure chest to your prospect. Understand that your Chest of Wonder is not designed for you to instantly win — it's designed to build emotional relevancy with your prospect, while slowly but surely building credibility. All the while causing curiosity to the point of driving an extreme perception of "missing out" if they don't take time to speak with you. This is about being present on all fronts.

Don't fall victim to the trap of thoughtless action as the foundation of your daily prospecting habits. Instead, fill your Chest with treasures designed to intentionally draw out your prospect and cause an Awakening.

TAKE A FEW MOMENTS AND REFLECT ON THE QUOTE AT THE BEGINNING OF THE DAY...

TODAY'S ADVENTURE

Start building your Chest of Wonder.

THE WARRIOR'S WORDS:

Let's talk about the FTPs inside your Chest of Wonder.

- **The Coffee-Stained Letter** - A marketing piece focused around a buyer being inundated by spam and sales garbage. It addresses the problem with the typical marketing ploys and, in doing so, interrupts the daily grind just enough that they focus on you for a moment. They will laugh, they will smirk, they will remember you.
- **The Not-So-Business Card** - This piece is actually the be-all and end-all for me in most cases. The front is a pretty wacky/fun scenario in which I'm placed with my product causing humor in the eye of the beholder, which builds on familiarity and relevance. Use pop culture, nostalgic messaging, and cause an emotional stir. For example: stand next to Chuck Norris as he roundhouse kicks the product you support, with text reading "Your Problems Don't Stand a Chance."
- **Your TV Commercials** - Don't worry, it doesn't have to air on TV, you can shoot it with your phone for all I care. This is your way of evolving with the times. Shoot something fun and relevant that builds credibility — again, focus on being a pattern interrupt to the market you're selling into. Put it on YouTube and promote it through email, social, and printed materials pointing people back to their smartphone to view your masterpiece. Also, there are great tools online that are free, or have a minimal cost in order to give you the power to edit and brand your videos to look professional. Or you can hit up the local agency that shoots video and go ALL-IN!
- **Product First Aid Kit** - Send your prospect a first aid kit full of all the pain points you want to address with them that your product can fix. Imagine the "Copier First Aid Kit" as an example. You'll put 4–5 items all labeled with numbers on them inside the kit, and a notecard that is branded to go along with them. The notecard has instructions as to what each item stands for (i.e. the band-aid is for wounds inflicted by the copier, such as paper cuts, scrapes caused by clearing a jam, etc).

DAY 18 — REFEREE'S HAND-BOOK

CONFUCIUS

"He who wishes to secure the good of others, has already secured his own."

Referrals from a satisfied client or a powerful networking relationship are some of the absolute best sales leads that exist. But getting referrals should be looked at as more personal than just trading leads in a networking group. Referrals represent trust, integrity, community, and so much more. Why? Because they come from an individual who believes in the work that you do. Because you've set the bar high and caused change within their business that cannot be replicated by just any vendor or product.

So, with an understanding of referrals from this perspective, we begin to recognize that they're something to be earned. Something genuine, something with exponential value. Quite naturally, something as exceptional as referrals, with all of their benefits, have their own cost. The trade out requires good communication, going the extra mile or five, and being willing to admit that you might not always be the right fit.

Understand that, NO MATTER WHAT, only a small minority of your clients will have you top of mind at all times for referrals. That's even if everyone is incredibly satisfied with your services. Let's not kid ourselves, it's just a fact.

Ultimately, referrals are an intricate piece of the puzzle in a successful sales career. In order to earn them, you have to be your absolute best and your client has to trust you. Because of this, service and integrity must be at the forefront of your existence. Earning a referral sharpens you on all fronts. It's not just about growing your business, it's about being a better person and professional to your clients. Some companies do such great work that they operate strictly through referrals — consider that for a moment.

"My Heart Longs to Learn and Aches to Serve" does yours?

TAKE A FEW MOMENTS AND REFLECT ON THE QUOTE AT THE BEGINNING OF THE DAY...

TODAY'S ADVENTURE

Go through your customer list and pick a few that you can run the exercise mentioned in today's Warrior's Words. Research your customers' products and be prepared to line up proper introductions for them as well.

THE WARRIOR'S WORDS:

Remember, an important aspect to referrals is recognizing that it's not all about you. You should practice what you preach by giving referrals to people you know who do excellent work, as you are expecting your clients and networks to do for you. I'm a power player in my accountant's (Bernie LeFils) networking circle. I've probably given him well over 40+ referrals because he's someone I trust to do good work for my trusted circle. I believe it with all my heart and expect nothing back from him outside of the excellent care he will take of the folks I send him. This is the attitude in which you expect the folks you serve to have about you, so live it.

For this one, I want you to build a super cool survey thingy... I know what you're thinking. But it's not that hard.

Start with a very well crafted design utilizing your brand and content, which shows 5 important questions to your client and asks them about specific services you're providing.

Now, place the numbers 1-5, individually, on the page under each question, and go visit your customer.

Ask them to rate each item based on their satisfaction so far.

This does two things:

#1: Allows you to fight off any issues early on in your relationship, or throughout your relationship, with the client (don't lie to yourself, problems can absolutely exist in any sale).

#2: If they give you a bunch of 4's and 5's, it indicates they trust you and you have earned credibility. Next, create a marketing piece that will go in your Chest of Wonder.

The objective here is a high-level conversation with your prospect about helping you to grow your business while doing your best to help them grow theirs.

Also remember, at the very least, providing them with a gift card to one of the local coffee shops for their time is respected. Rewarding your champions will go a long way if done using integrity and the mindset of a servant leader.

DAY 19

CURIOSITY... WHAT?

ANATOLE FRANCE

"The whole art of teaching is only the art of awakening the natural curiosity of young minds for the purpose of satisfying it afterwards..."

As a Rebel, curiosity should be the first major ingredient in all of your prospecting activities. It's followed by getting your prospect's attention, interrupting their normal patterns, and knowing your prospect and their business better. You also have to be curious in order to learn the truths of your prospect.

Let's talk about approaching your decision maker indirectly. Start with his/her employees and get to know the company by better understanding the roles that are essential to its operations.

How does a Rebel learn more about said roles...let's find out!

Reception. I know what you're thinking... *window witch, vice president of no, my worst nightmare, Gatekeeper.* Well, get over yourself, the person at the front desk gives you a hard time because you suck and always waste their time with your self-involved crappy sales pitch that they've heard from 50 other people this week. If you want to be the change in your industry, then start acting like it.

Once you've started building relationships inside of an organization, you can truly start to learn more about the firm from a completely different viewpoint. Imagine the power behind meeting with a decision maker and being able to tell him/her about the problems their firm is experiencing because you have literally heard them from the source.

Now you can nuance the R.E.A.S.O.N. methodology of calling the C-level executive you're seeking a meeting with. You are literally setting yourself up for a slam dunk introduction. Imagine calling back the same receptionist and saying, "Hey! It's The Copier Warrior, how are you!? It's good to talk to you again. Were you able to get my Crumpled Letter back to the boss and are they available today?" They'll pass you straight back and they will tee you up as well. Because you are surrounding the business and focusing on what no other salesperson does at this point — a relationship with non-decision makers, and the curiosity and attention of the buyer.

This is how you come to K.N.O.W. the prospect and how you get on another level with them. Taking time to learn more about your prospects and their current situation in order to do more than help them "save some money" on your widget — this is a method of surrounding the business and taking a stake in more than just the decision maker and his/her signature.

It's important to understand all the knowledge of your product amounts to nothing when your prospect doesn't care about what you're selling. Especially when they're sick and tired of dealing with the same old self-serving salespeople in the first place.

So remember... this day is about seeing the bigger picture from someone else's point of view and giving yourself an advantage when exercising the R.E.A.S.O.N. method and understanding the K.N.O.W. theory. This is all about bridging the emotional gap and creating interest. It's about speaking to your prospect using their language, not yours. The language of listening by engaging with those who surround and have influence with the decision maker.

Like a true Sales Rebel.

TAKE A FEW MOMENTS AND REFLECT ON THE QUOTE AT THE BEGINNING OF THE DAY...

┌─TODAY'S ADVENTURE─┐

Start with an existing customer where you only know the decision maker and their assistant. Go meet others in the firm and learn more about what's important to them.

THE WARRIOR'S WORDS:

Here's the mindset and example for the introduction you are about to make: "Before I say anything else, will you promise not to punch me right in the face when I tell you what I do? Because I'm a sales guy... but you knew that before I even walked through the door — we have a very specific smell. However, I hope to help you see that I'm not like anything that has ever come through that front door. Today, I just wanted to say 'hi' and leave this with you (hand off a Crumpled Letter) because I know that in order to meet with the CFO who makes decisions on the products and services I provide, *you* have to trust me. I also know that you have your finger on the pulse of this organization — all the good, all the bad, all the problems pertaining to the widget I sell, everything. So, I'm here to earn it, if you'll let me."

DAY 20 YOUR REBELLION

ANDRE MAURIOS

"*Either the soul is eternal and we shall not die, or it perishes with the flesh, and we shall not know that we are dead. Live, then, as if you were eternal.*"

Crazy week, huh? Welcome to your Rebellion! What this book has been teaching you, cannot be looked at as the "norm" in the sales world... But the new world will be made of these unconventional methods. They're not popular, true. However, this is because sales, and its leaders, have cultured a system where salespeople work for the product/service and not the other way around. The Sales Rebellion believe that change is inevitable. And the Rebellion intends to equip a movement that will breathe life into the next generation.

Your pipeline is alive, your prospects have a pulse, your processes are not a pre-programmed function of a CB-1-2-MANY, your Chest of Wonder is more than brochures and white papers, your prospecting has a R.E.A.S.O.N., your business is being built and not bought. Beginning to see the picture yet? Can you feel the difference this will make?

Many people in the sales world see much of this as weakness. "Just cash the check and move on," they say. "Just bother them until they take a meeting with you. Just tell them they owe you a reference letter. Just separate your business life from your personal life." Et cetera, et cetera.

Yes... If we're being honest, no matter how bad we're making it sound, we would rather do it the old way. It's easier... there's less of an investment. We don't have to search deep within ourselves, we don't have to have feelings or process emotion. We like it when service is a department and not an action, it's just easier... but is it fulfilling?

Does it truly serve the betterment of your community and those whom you interact with on a daily basis? Does winning a new account hit you deep in your soul and cause an emotional awakening because you see the true purpose of your existence? Does it energize you when you make genuine connections with others, or does it feel like you're one step closer to a bigger commission check? Are you *truly* living? Are you helping others truly live? Are you Rebelling against the status quo?

Remember short term rewards have no meaning in comparison to the bigger picture, the eternal picture. In other words, we recognize that even after we're gone from this earth it continues spinning with a new set of people living on it. Thus, Legacies are about having such an impact on the people around you that they can't help but share with others the ways in which they connect with you. This type of sales is about real life. It's about connection and intentionality, and it has a focus on the long run. It's innovative, not fully explored, maybe, a bit mysterious and confusing. But it is undoubtedly the future of the sales industry. Are you willing to search? Are you willing to think, or have you stopped reading already? Will you walk this earth already dead, a naysayer? Or, will you choose to immerse others in your Legacy?

TAKE A FEW MOMENTS AND REFLECT ON THE QUOTE AT THE BEGINNING OF THE DAY...

TODAY'S ADVENTURE

Look back over the last week and decide what the most important piece to your future is. Then decide how it can be implemented into your daily life. Write it down and do it without excuses.

_____
_____
_____
_____
_____
_____
_____
_____
_____
_____
_____
_____
_____
_____
_____
_____
_____
_____
_____
_____
_____
_____
_____
_____
_____
_____

DAY 21 ACTION ITEMS

EDWARD EVERETT HALE

"I am only one
But still I am one.
I cannot do everything,
But still I can do something;
And because I cannot do everything
I will not refuse to do the something that I can do."

The Sales Rebellion believes Sundays are for giving back. This action is about the fulfillment of your role as a servant to your community. This is a sacred day for some of you who have been following along with us day by day, and we're thankful for that.

When we look at the Roots of The Copier Warrior's sales walk, service is an important part of his outlook. Now think about The Living Pipeline. In order to fully mature and nurture each branch, you must start by feeding the Roots. Without them, there is no Chest of Wonder, there is no R.E.A.S.O.N., there are no branches, there is no fruit.

Maybe you're having a hard time truly understanding the need for this attitude geared toward giving back. Servant leadership is not necessarily an easy concept to grasp and execute on a daily basis. It requires empathy to the nth degree. Maybe you don't know what it's like to swipe a government-assisted credit card at the store. Maybe you don't know the experience of not having a bed to rest your head on at the end of a long day, and by the grace of God, you never will.

Service is about more than helping people. It's about sharing the burden, even when it's an emotional one. So, walk a mile in their shoes. This week, it's all about understanding what hardship looks like and the difficult things people are dealing with in their lives. This is the pain and sorrow side of life. Don't be mad at the receptionist for being rude to you during a prospecting call. Instead, think about the hardships she or he might possibly be experiencing and show compassion to, and for them no matter what. Experience all aspects of life and open yourself up to the realities of other human beings.

Go a step further in your giving this week and experience empathy. Open your heart and listen.

TAKE A FEW MOMENTS AND REFLECT ON THE QUOTE AT THE BEGINNING OF THE DAY...

TODAY'S ADVENTURE

Grab a sleeping bag and head down to the local homeless shelter to fellowship, learn, and immerse yourself. Maybe, even spend the night. Walk 2 miles instead of 1. Gasping in disbelief? Then go down to the local Boys and Girls Club and sign up to be a volunteer. The point is to intentionally experience empathy. **Go.**

DAY 22
CLOSE YOUR DAY AT A HOTEL

HELEN KELLER

"I long to accomplish a great and noble task, but it is my chief duty to accomplish small tasks as if they were great and noble."

Picking up where we left off last... It's around 1:00 pm and now that your belly is as full as your heart, it's time to get back to work. But, don't let the word "work" deflate your balloon— because back at the office lies immeasurable growth and success.

Yes, it's time to check-in on all the first touch pieces you have left your new prospects from earlier in the morning. There's a dual process here... calling and emailing behind your marketing drops/engagements, and gaining momentum by appropriately re-engaging.

By now, your FTP should have made its way to the key contact you're attracting. So, buckle up... it's time for the follow-up! Remember, a good warm drop allows you to break down barriers at the front desk and provides a window for building rapport. So, when you call, it should sound like this: "Hey, it's *insert your name* from earlier. It was awesome meeting you. I'm calling real quick to see if John Doe had a minute to talk now that he's gotten my Crumpled Letter." When you speak, continue to lead with confidence and be intentional with your words when talking to the front desk. Help them to believe you're not a CB-1-2-MANY.

Once you get your key connection on the phone, it's time to bust open the cap on your homemade sauce. Turn doubt into curiosity, get them ready for their Awakening, and lead them into your Rebellion. This is follow-up — Rebellicious style!

Once you've made it through your drop list from the day, start doing follow-up calls and emails into the branches of your Living Pipeline. Remember the following word when doing your follow-ups — intentionality. The reason it's important to be intentional in your actions is it requires you to stay focused. And, when you're focused, you can be much more aware of the opportunities around you. Head into your 30/60/90/120 branch, check-in with your 12-month branch, make a phone call or put something in the mail to your Wild Cards, send a piece of content to the folks in your 2-year branch. Think of this time as impactful to the folks you are cultivating credibility with. You're watering the seeds you have worked so hard to cultivate.

After a few hours of checking in on your drops and nurturing your Living Pipeline, it should be getting close to 5:00 pm, the end of the day. This is a blink of the eye in your day, but a very important blink. Make sure you've engaged with everyone internally on your team regarding any projects that are currently open. Thank the logistics folks for any completed jobs they have closed out, shoot an email to management praising someone at the office who went above and beyond for you recently. This is a moment where you can further grow your relationships internally within the office.

You can also use this time to send a similar type of email to the folks you're networking with in the community. Take a minute to do some introductions to said referral partners. You can even take this time to write a quick thank you card (hand-written) to someone who gave you a warm intro to a new client. The point is, use this time to continue to make your mark. It's important these things are all wrapped up. So tomorrow, with no distractions, you can conquer once again.

Now, before you make your exit for the day, make one more

call. That's the Rebel way. There are some popular ideas behind this: like the sticky note on a light switch method or a calendar reminder every day at 5:15 p.m. that says "ONE MORE CALL." But let's be honest, you dial and nobody is in, then you end up just going home anyway. You pat yourself on the back for a job well done. Your "one more call" really accomplished a lot... can you feel the sarcasm being laid on here?

Pro Tip:
Your habits and rhythms become the power of your presence and are what constitute you being relevant to your community.

This day is all about how habits and rhythms sculpt our outcomes. A structure allows us to apply everything in your Chest of Wonder to a workflow that will cultivate your Living Pipeline. The notion of making calls after-hours is not about having a habit of making fruitless calls to prospects that don't answer anyway. After-hour calls are merely a concept from the wisdom of a Rebel Copier Warrior who once had nothing, but gained everything by thinking outside the box.

Long to complete your great and mighty tasks and allow them to bring joy into your routine. A happy work-life starts with doing what you love.

TAKE A FEW MOMENTS AND REFLECT ON THE QUOTE AT THE BEGINNING OF THE DAY...

TODAY'S ADVENTURE

Cold call someone after 5:00 p.m.

THE WARRIOR'S WORDS:

My cadences started out with me doing drops from 8:00 am – 5:00 pm every day for both Monday and Tuesday. By Wednesday, I would pivot to leaving my drops in the morning to lunch hours and then getting on the phone. In my first week, by Wednesday, I had about 100 people to call and follow-up with from all the FTP drops I had done. This creates an appropriate amount of work for yourself as you continue to evolve into working smarter alongside working harder.

Now, let's try something new that will actually get someone to engage with you. Get in the car and head to a hotel.

> **Disclaimer:** if you're not in an industry that sells to hotels then I would challenge you to think outside the box and figure out what industry you could uniquely call on in an after-hours manner. The example below demonstrates a unique cold call that grabs attention, builds wonder, disarms with humor, and closes with a call to action.

Your Hotel stop-in should look something like this when done after-hours:

- Head straight to the bar and order a Sprite with a lime. Hopefully, there are a few people there so you can spark up some fellowship. If not, the bartender becomes your "gatekeeper" for the evening. So, just go ahead and work on your rapport with her/him solely.
- After downing your first Sprite and lime, ask the bartender if they wouldn't mind getting the General Manager of the Hotel or the AGM (whoever is on the clock at this hour).
- When they arrive, your conversation should sound something like this: "Thanks for coming out to meet me (then introduce yourself) — I know most of the time that someone asks for you, it's usually followed by a complaint. So, just wanted to take a second and compliment you on the great job you're doing here. This drink was delicious and your staff has treated me with kindness (don't lie about these things, change your talk track if both of those subjects sucked). Wanted to also let you know I'm a member of the local business community here."

- "Wanted to leave this with you and see if we could connect on LinkedIn and stay in touch. Would love to come back at a better time to take a tour of the facility and find out more about how you're using (insert the widget you sell here)."

These are the basics behind how to make an initial call, after-hours, to a prospect such as the infamous hotel manager. Remember, calling on a hotel after 5 pm to sell your services is a pattern interrupt. The above outline as a script should be sufficient enough as a starting line for you. Allow your curiosity to blossom by thinking through all the intentional ways you can decorate this call to the prospect. The marketing piece that I addressed goes along with the Legend you're building in the community. It's humorous, it's tailored to the vertical, and ignites the brain to fire on all cylinders in order to ace the first call and start building a relationship with your new contact.

You can find a workflow and an outline for the structure behind this interaction with your decision maker in the R.E.A.S.O.N. curriculum. Go sign up for the course!

DAY 23 TERRITORY PART 4

──── **RALPH WALDO EMERSON** ────

"We take care of our health, we lay up money, we make our roof tight and our clothing sufficient, but who provides wisely that he shall not be wanting in the best property of all — friends."

The Sales Rebellion loves the subject of Territory. Through these teachings, we've turned it upside down and taught you how to take all the things you *thought* were true about "sales" and toss them. You have learned about theories behind structuring your curated lists appropriately, how to build your Living Pipeline, etc. Now it's time to dive deeper into the individual businesses that hang from one of your many branches. Let's talk about how we expand our territory through one single contact — the decision maker.

The decision maker at a business is the next and final part of territory as it pertains to this section. You have to realize that the decision maker, inside of your territory, inside the business you are seeking to serve, is a territory in and of itself. Eat your heart out *Inception*.

Where do they golf, where do they get an evening drink or their morning coffee, what is their culture? Have you realized that they're a living breathing advertisement for you as well? A warm introduction to all their business colleagues is certainly attainable if we're focused on earning it. Understand that each individual you encounter has his, or her own circles of influence. Each has a long list of contacts that you've been trying to meet, or didn't know existed in the first place.

The decision maker as a territory is hard to comprehend for some folks... so just think about their routines. They show up at the same local coffee shop every morning at 7:30 a.m., and order the cold brew with oat milk — in fact, they don't even ask for their order because the barista already knows. When they grab lunch, it's usually at the same mom and pop restaurant where they know the owner's son. They went to school together. Incidentally, all the servers know the name of your decision maker and the chef is already fixing up their club sandwich before they sit down. Do you get the picture?

These people love their community and are incredibly involved in it. Furthermore, their community loves them back. They are the "gatekeeper" to a plethora of new connections to which they will warmly introduce you... if you earn it.

When you identify them through your prospecting, approach them in a manner they would appreciate. Use a Tool from your Chest of Wonder to convey the importance of your culture and how you provide experiences for the people you work with. Stay focused on the much larger picture of quality introductions and a really epic reference letter that will make everyone jealous! Have a mentality where, even if you're not able to help them with your products and services, they can still be one of your greatest allies, and vice versa! Go deeper into your territory with this mindset.

Your Territory is a living, breathing thing. It is bigger than you have allowed it to be. It has more meaning than you have allowed it to have. If salespeople would stop looking at everyone and everything as a "sale", the world would be a far better place.

Think back to the first friend you ever made. Think about the innocence in your interactions — you were curious, your heart full of love. Another human, like you, living their life alongside yours on the playground until it was time to go home. Your friends are people with which you enjoy the raw human influx of emotions and building relationship together. Look at your prospect the same way, in the most innocent way. Romanticize your business relationship with them.

Take your attitude, your R.E.A.S.O.N. all that we've learned about service, networking, your Living Pipeline, and apply it to the territory that resides within your prospects and clients. Go after your prospect with a whole new outlook. Understand *why* it's so important to build credibility for a bigger purpose than just getting the paperwork signed and cashing the check.

The key is to revolutionize the way you perceive your territory. It is a land of fun, friendships, and financial successes for both you and your prospects! Because you're nothing in this world without true connections that translate into real value for both parties. Not just through products and services, but in the name of success. This way, when you have taken your last breath, and left this earthly shell, your community will look back upon all you've done and they'll be proud to have called you, friend.

TAKE A FEW MOMENTS AND REFLECT ON THE QUOTE AT THE BEGINNING OF THE DAY...

TODAY'S ADVENTURE

Learn more about your decision maker. Get to know their circles and become more involved in their culture.

THE WARRIOR'S WORDS:

I was golfing with a decision maker/friend of mine. He brought a guest and I brought a guest. The gentleman he brought along worked for a manufacturing company that made one single part for a company that would buy $5–$10 million a year. They literally did not do ANYTHING else but make this one part. Their building was not that big — a few machines inside, 100 employees, in the middle of nowhere and it looked like an abandoned warehouse. I would have never thought... in fact, I would've never known, had I not met that gentleman on the greens that day. I suck at golf, by the way... but I digress. Are you applying this idea in your head yet? We all have our circles — go find the ones you're not a part of.

One of my mentors, Steve Nudelberg, once sent out a first touch piece with his marketing agency that got him on the phone with each and every one of his prospects. There was a catch — one of them told him he would NEVER buy from him, but to fly up and meet him, because he will be the single best source of business for him and his firm! The gentleman NEVER bought from him, as promised, but he got him more business than he knew what to do with. Check out *Confessions of A Serial Salesman* by Steve to learn more about his audacious and successful sales walk.

Another friend of mine in Central FL, Dusty Rollins, has a networking group where he puts a meeting together full of business owners that trust him, whom he has built a culture of community with. If Dusty invited you to that event, you would meet a dozen new power players that could either use, and make decisions on the products and services you provide, or refer you to some of the most profitable businesses you've ever encountered. You would never know about this group if you were out targeting decision makers like Dusty just to get him to buy from you. His perception of you would stay solely focused on you being in sales, and him having a need for your product in which he is going to bid you out against 3 other vendors, nothing more.

So, approach people with a learning attitude and get ready to enjoy the bountiful fruit that blooms from it.

DAY 24
LEVEL 60 DELTA MOMENTS

JAMES FRAZER

"The world cannot live at the level of its great men."

If you look back to the beginning of our journey, you'll notice that we started with a simple concept — the idea of building your Roots and practicing your R.E.A.S.O.N. Here, on our final discussion about prospecting, you're going to get some Delta Moment ideas that'll rock your prospect until the break of dawn, give you a little taste of the unique idea department, and will hopefully blow your flippin' mind!

So, we've discussed Roots and R.E.A.S.O.N., targeted cold calls, and some good basic principles behind prospecting. Now, let's discuss one of The Copier Warrior's favorite ideas behind learning more about a business from the horse's mouth. All the while, cultivating a referral relationship with someone at the business you're wanting to set an appointment with.

Today you're going to call on the sales department at a business that you have been denied and rejected multiple times to date — Rebel style!

The concept here is to align yourself with someone in the same role as you inside the firm you're hoping to serve. This individual, as a salesperson, should absolutely be interested in meeting with you, and will be a great source of knowledge to you in regards to the firm they work for. They will also love the novelty of the whole thing and might even tell you, "this has never happened to me before," further continuing your journey.

Understand too, it's important to pick a vertical in which you can truly align yourself with the sales rep you meet. What if your products and services are the wrong fit for the firm? And remember, the true focus here is on whether or not you can help this salesperson with referrals and earn some of your own. It's not *just* about getting one step closer to the account. Now the interaction has a real purpose. This is your Delta.

Next, we want you to think about the biggest and baddest account in your territory. One that is intimidating to call on in any capacity. Their front door is HID-card access only, the front desk has to buzz you in after you talk to them through an intercom, a really awkward in-person call... because of this, you dial them. The receptionist always answers pleasantly (I think she likes me!) then pushes you back to the extension of the decision maker (Oh, she really like me!), you leave a voicemail (Yes, victory over the cold call)! Except the line you were transferred to is the voicemail they set up for solicitors Just. Like. You. Congrats, you're now in voicemail jail. No one cares, and there's no card that gets you out for free.

So, rather than being condemned to voicemail jail for the rest of your career... try this:

- Head down to the office, push the buzzer, and tell the front desk "I have a package for Mr./Mrs. Smith."
- Walk through the front door holding a 6'0" (life-sized) cardboard cutout of yourself. Have fun with the pose and any props you want in the picture/cutout
- Place it with the front desk and ask them to please deliver it for you
- Place a call to action on your cutout that relates to curiosity, relevance, and an impactful message that dares them to reach out

- They'll be so confused and so in love all at the same time, that there will be an odd attraction about what it is you are trying to accomplish
- Naturally, questions will flow
- Tell the story of the pains they are experiencing by not having your expertise/product. A story for the ages, one that will be ingrained into the relationship you are cultivating with your new friend
- Enjoy this Delta Moment to its fullest

Now, once you're back at your office, make that same phone call you've done a thousand times. Tell the front desk who you are, "I dropped off the big cutout of my ugly mug for Mr./Mrs. Smith," then breathe out as she presses hold, and connects you to the actual decision maker... buckle up you're about to speak with the long-awaited human you've been seeking to have a conversation with.

Understand that when you're creating this addition to your Chest of Wonder, you need to be focused on your R.E.A.S.O.N. Because what it communicates is far more important than the fact that it's a giant cutout of yourself.

Let's dive deeper using a Rebel mindset and ideas... imagine your Google Alerts sent you a notification about a new ribbon-cutting in the area, and your relationship with the local EDC has helped you to understand more about the organization, and *why* they're opening their doors in your community. Instead of calling on them to offer your products and services, get a head-count of the total employees, call your local catering vendor (one you should have a referral relationship with, by the way), and take lunch down to your new neighbor.

Create a Tool in your Chest of Wonder that sticks to the utensils/paper plates while conveying your R.E.A.S.O.N. and welcomes them to their new community — remember to further your brand and get people curious over how intentional you are. When you do this, the owner of the company will literally come out to shake your hand. You should welcome them to the area and convey you're here to help. Whether that means meeting more of the neighbors or providing your services to their firm. Focus on them and how you can be of service — the foundation of a fruitful business relationship.

Be genuine with this approach. If you cannot get behind the idea that they might already have someone who provides your products or services and they don't need you, then everything you're working to attract here will be lost.

You want the owner to walk back to their desk and think "I need to keep this person close" to some capacity. Because it's more about who you are... than what you sell. Remember the territory inside the territory (INCEPTION REFERRALS through the C-Suite). Do not disregard the power of relationships built through credibility, and how intentional actions affect the long term goals you're pursuing. This is a multi-level Delta Moment that should cause a deep stir inside your very being.

Now, for the grand finale. Call up the local marketing/PR firm and get a discovery session put together. Tell them you're seeking to work with 10 businesses in the area, different verticals, all of the folks you deem as "High-Value Alliances" whether they're big or small. After you're done brainstorming and creating the campaign, hit the streets with a couple of zombies, or body builders, or Star Wars characters and take your script to their front doors/parking lots/street corners and get the campaign rolling! You need visual branding, signage being carried, flyers, and marketing being passed out themed to the campaign with a call to action toward your products and services.

Prospecting is all about the eventual Delta Moments. It's also about humanizing the process and understanding that your prospects are NORMAL PEOPLE who go to concerts on the weekend, watch Netflix at the end of the day, and head to Wine-Down-Wednesday with their friends. So, we work hard to build a culture of friendships and community in order to further pursue greatness, and to connect with those we encounter on a more meaningful level.

Throughout this journey, we're allowed the opportunity to shine brighter than the sun. It's our choice in whether or not we accept the challenge, but the duty remains the same. It is your duty to #ChangeTheGame.

TAKE A FEW MOMENTS AND REFLECT ON THE QUOTE AT THE BEGINNING OF THE DAY...

TODAY'S ADVENTURE

Have a side of Delta Moments with your coffee stains this morning...

THE WARRIOR'S WORDS:

Here's my script/mentality behind calling on the sales department of a company you've been wanting to serve:

> *"Hey Jack/Jill, my name's Dale. I'm the Leader of The Sales Rebellion, a local firm here in the area, and thought you and I could grab a coffee and talk more about our sales goals and what businesses we're seeking to serve . We can share some war stories and have a therapy moment as well because sales can suck and we both know how important a little positivity and camaraderie is from time to time."*

Additionally, here's the scoop on tough to reach businesses. Sometimes, there will be businesses that are on full lockdown and won't even have a buzzer like this. When this happens, your SDR/BDR skills have to kick in and you've got to work your way through LinkedIn profiles, Instagram users, Facebook messages, and the PHONE — the last thing you wanted to hear me say, I know (unless you are an SDR/BDR!)

Video comes in handy when breaking through to these types of accounts. Don't forget that you can TEXT a full-fledged video introduction to a point of contact, message it to them on Instagram, or even Facebook and LinkedIn. There are basically no excuses to NOT use technology these days. You can interrupt the normal patterns of your buyer, relay authenticity, instill curiosity, and create a fun and enjoyable first touch: all through social channels and utilizing the phone as needed.

DAY 23

THE SALESPERSON AND THEIR COMMUNITY

2 CHRONICLES 31:21

"He did it with all his heart, and prospered."

It's important to know that a Rebellion will help you to better understand networking and referrals in their true and natural state. At the root of all these activities has been an underlying theme of giving without gain. Naturally, you'll absolutely be rewarded by some form of fruit, but the attitude walking in is: "I do this because I am."

Today, ask yourself, what am I passionate about? What would I find absolute joy in doing as an act of service/kindness in my community? Let's look at service opportunities together.

One of the easiest ways to serve is by giving your own personal time or making a financial contribution. Yet always remember that your time is worth more than any dollar amount. Another easy practice is to look up one of the larger organizations that might have a footprint in your area such as The Red Cross, Salvation Army, Goodwill, etc. These are all outstanding organizations and should definitely be considered when you're choosing who you'll get involved with.

But remember, there are people on a much smaller scale, having a much larger impact in your own backyard. Keep in mind that these types of financial contributions can lead to business opportunities by putting your name on the sponsor list for an upcoming event. They can stick your logo on a t-shirt for the upcoming 5K, or even host the upcoming luncheon which will give you a chance to educate others on your products, services, and culture.

A good example of a locally run charity is The Children's Hunger Network in Brevard County. These folks are feeding kids through our school systems in which over 50% are on a free or reduced-price meal program because their parents are not able to afford to feed them. Even though the schools are providing nutrition, when the weekend hits, these kids go hungry.

This group goes above and beyond, providing nutrition through the weekend. Because of this, they need volunteers to come and pack lunches. They also need donations in order to continue to buy the food, in which they give away, at no charge to these children in need. So spend a few hours packing food for the next generation and prove you'll invest in their future. Don't forget why we're getting involved. You are in sales to serve.

Consider heading over to the Boys and Girls Club, or Big Brothers Big Sisters, and learn about how they develop our youth to have a more positive outlook on their future — one that encourages them to dream big and work hard to earn their successes. You can give your personal time in order to help develop these young men and women. Some of them are aspiring to become engineers, others as public servants, while many have the desire to become entrepreneurs. All kinds of unique aspirations and big dreams. These are young minds. Think of what the benefits would've been to you in your professional and personal walk, if you had a mentor at such a young age who was intentionally setting an example for you and proactively guiding you in your journey to success. Powerful Legacy here Rebels.

There are opportunities to sponsor yearly galas/events that act as fundraisers and help bring the local businessmen and women together in celebration of these organizations. Fellowship with your peers and colleagues is healthy. Enjoying the fruits of your kindness, and recognizing now that you're making a huge impact on the future of your community is also a healthy way to serve. Remember that through these types of events you are able to continue building your legend, earn credibility, and truly bond with the business leaders around you. Bring your significant other or a family member with you. This is a natural and fun way to build a culture of friendship with the businesses in your community. It's the culture of a Rebel.

Another opportunity would be to meet the director at your local non-profit and learn more about the board of directors. Learn how you can be more deeply involved by serving with that group of individuals who are making an impact behind the scenes. There's nothing like giving your personal time to the overall organization's operation, through feedback and governance, with a group of like-minded business leaders. A Board of Directors is very important to the existence of a local non-profit. They help with the budgets, planning events, thinking outside the box — overcoming daily obstacles both big and small.They'll connect you to other business leaders in your community as well, and allow them to get a different glimpse into who you truly are. Remember, one of the goals of this book is to help you understand how trust is given... through credibility.

So remember, prosperity is not bought, it's built. Do not look at service as a shortcut — you will reach a dead end. Instead, give back. Use your gifts to bless others and help them see they have the exact same potential to make an impact. The grass is only greener if you water it.

TAKE A FEW MOMENTS AND REFLECT ON THE QUOTE AT THE BEGINNING OF THE DAY...

TODAY'S ADVENTURE

Think about how you fit into your community. The relationships are there if you are actively participating. Begin practicing your leadership locally.

THE WARRIOR'S WORDS:

To unite with others around a cause that is noble, one that brings light to circumstances that can be overcome if they are put under a spotlight and not avoided... it's one of the greatest pieces of fulfillment your soul will find in your walk on this earth.

DAY 26
THE PRODUCT OF KNOWLEDGE

WALT WHITMAN

"Wisdom is not finally tested in the schools,
Wisdom cannot be passed from one having it to another not having it,
Wisdom is of the soul, is not susceptible of proof, is its own proof."

The K.N.O.W. theory should be one of your favorite subjects at this point. Most of us look at knowledge differently, but the majority of salespeople focus mainly on product features and the talk tracks to convey their benefits and advantages... Well, today we're going to "sell out" and talk about just that. But don't worry, there's a twist! There's always a twist when you're starting a Rebellion.

Product knowledge is not the features, advantages, and benefits of your offering. It is not based around a two-hour weekly session with your training department either. Furthermore, it's not how well you can present the brochure or dog + pony the widget's key talking points. It's about wherewithal, and a greater understanding of how your widget will work inside of those four walls. It's the kind of knowledge you learn in the streets through experience and over time.

So, to educate yourself through the hands-on-method without having to invent a time machine, let's call up a support person in your company and spend a day in the field with them. This will help you better understand what it looks like to go from call to call, the issues they deal with for your clients, the culture of customer service, and the very distinct relationship that your service/customer support department has with your client.

Also, hang out with the billing department so you can watch their 8 hour day and understand your industry through their eyes and how your clients interact with them. Next, go along with the corporate trainer to a few installs and watch all the different questions fly around the room, learn what is important to certain verticals, and gain some next-level knowledge on questions that will sharpen you and the solutions you provide.

Let's illustrate this point a different way... Do you know why golfers scream "fore" when they hit the ball toward a group of people? Or do you just know that golfers say "fore?" A "fore-caddie" was an individual that would stand downrange during a golf game to watch where the ball would land. A golfer would yell "fore-caddie" which was eventually shortened to "fore" after they would hit the ball in the direction of that individual. You have been yelling "fore" at people instead of "WATCH OUT, MY BALL IS TRAVELING AT YOUR FACE" for years and never knew what "fore" actually meant until this very moment. You're welcome. LIfe changing knowledge Rebels.

The principle behind this learning moment? Not everything is as it seems. The real reason we say "fore" has an interesting story attached to it, just like your products and services can, along with the reason they're used by your marketplace. What's on the surface is a plain old boring word that doesn't even make any sense!

So, do you know why your customers buy your products and services? Or are you just blindly yelling "FORE!"

Embrace the idea of there being a greater purpose behind being in the K.N.O.W. One that connects deep within your own soul. A why.

TAKE A FEW MOMENTS AND REFLECT ON THE QUOTE AT THE BEGINNING OF THE DAY...

TODAY'S ADVENTURE

Sharpen your street knowledge of the products and services you provide to the community. Instead of saying that an ROI on your low-cost product is the only value, recognize REAL value instead. Write down the areas you're weak. Commit to learning how your product works in three separate industries and not from your company's knowledge base — call the prospect! Ask them to explain what your product truly does for them.

_____

_____

_____

_____

_____

_____

_____

_____

_____

_____

_____

_____

_____

_____

_____

_____

THE WARRIOR'S WORDS:

At 10 years old, you could catch me at my dad's office. I was supposed to be cleaning or organizing, but, for the most part, you would catch me being a ladies man. Trying to impress all the wonderful women my father employed, playing hide and seek in the warehouse with my siblings, yucking it up with my favorite service techs that I believed were superheroes, and making copies or sending a fax — just because I knew how to do that. I learned through experience and, in my later years, you could find me answering the phones, logging service calls for dispatch. I always had a mental picture of exactly what was going on — how the copier worked, all the moving parts, all the major components, and all the reasons it could be breaking and how we could fix it — I saw it all. I saw it because I loved my father's business and I loved serving others. I loved... a word we have forgotten the true meaning of.

I was privileged to be born into and raised in the same industry where I built my career. That doesn't mean you can't have the same level of awareness and education as me. It means your attitude should be focused on getting the same experience in order to truly learn your products. You should be more focused on *why* your widget has this specific feature, and stop presenting it as a bullet point. Understand its impact deeply and meaningfully from a 360-degree point of view.

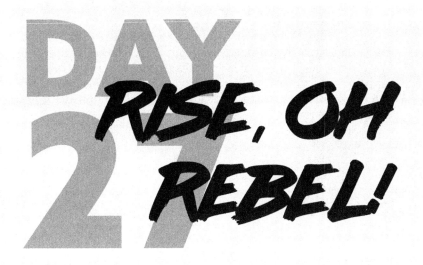

DAY 27
RISE, OH REBEL!

COLETTE

"What a wonderful life I've had! I only wish I'd realized it sooner."

All of life is perception. Don't compare yesterday against today, but rather imagine what tomorrow can be and envision the steps you must take to get there. Recognize that perceptions can be toxic when they cause you to carry doubt or envy in your heart. Allowing yourself to be living one foot in front of the other, causes you to always be solving the puzzle of life for the betterment of yourself and those around you. This type of attitude causes a ripple effect of hope.

Another piece of this equation is that most people seek the path of least resistance and never realize that it's the struggles and hardships that help build character and understanding. We perceive these experiences as "bad," and allow them to fester within our soul because we seek convenience and forget that true development doesn't always feel good. We look to experience the good and isolate everything else. But we need that everything else... without it, we only have a two-dimensional perspective of what life is. In other words, we can't have the highs without the lows.

145

While you reflect on this teaching, remember that perceptions can be our best friend... or our greatest enemy. In order to experience your Rebel awakening, you must understand that failure and rejection are learning tools for tomorrow. Move forward and perceive the greatness. You're called to greatness found in the exploration of the darkest valleys and the highest mountains. Go light your torch!

TAKE A FEW MOMENTS AND REFLECT ON THE QUOTE AT THE BEGINNING OF THE DAY...

TODAY'S ADVENTURE

Change your perception of failure. Take something in your life that you perceive to be negative and shine your light into it.

DAY 28
MAGNANIMOUS

THOMAS CARLYLE

"Do the duty which lies nearest thee... Thy second duty will already have become clearer."

By now it should be quite clear. The objective we should be most focused on during our journey is the success that we can provide to others through our actions, our products, our services, and our mindset. But there is one very important ingredient needed in order to carry this out. One we have not yet explored. That ingredient is YOU. In order to properly breathe life back into your community, you must know-thy-self. Today's topic of service is YOU and how you are developing yourself.

Consider how you can learn from people of all shapes and sizes that you encounter during your walk. Sometimes the best learning experiences are provided by the folks who are in the trenches actually doing the actual work, not an article on the internet. Consider the experiences that you don't know, nor will ever have. The best way to better understand is to "walk a mile in their shoes." Be creative about how you go about this.

The Copier Warrior has done ride-alongs with people in other sales verticals, sat inside of call centers and listened to inbound customer service issues, gone on-site, and experienced the daily grind through the eyes of a day-to-day employee that typically gets overlooked. These are all pieces to the puzzle.

Don't forget to continue developing yourself in the midst of serving your community. Continue to build an internal belief system in what you know and all you can accomplish. Use mornings, nights, weekends, and any other possible opportunity. Sharpen who you are personally, as a professional and as an individual member of the community you are supporting. You might think it sounds crazy, but the time you spend with your family and friends can be just as important in supporting the concept we are learning here. Every moment has the potential of being a unique experience that you can use to sharpen yourself and share with others. You just have to see it through the eyes of a Rebel.

TAKE A FEW MOMENTS AND REFLECT ON THE QUOTE AT THE BEGINNING OF THE DAY...

TODAY'S ADVENTURE

Honor your legacy, today. You owe it to yourself to be involved in your community. Walk around the block and say hello to the people that live in your neighborhood. Grab a pick-up game at the public basketball court, help someone carry their groceries to the car. It's that simple. Dare to live outside your comfort zone.

DAY 29
THE WARRIOR'S WORDS

MARTIN LUTHER KING JR.

"If a man is called to be a street sweeper, he should sweep the streets even as Michelangelo painted, or Beethoven composed music, or Shakespeare wrote poetry. He should sweep streets so well that all the hosts of heaven and earth will pause to say, here lived a great street sweeper who did his job well."

In life, we're given lessons through learning experiences and other people's ideas. In most cases, we usually forget them both. We talk the talk when reciting what we liked about something we learned, but rarely do we walk the walk. We're all guilty of it. It's the simple thought of applying and living by what we have gathered to be the truth, but it is not as easy as it sounds.

Selfishly, we like to think we already understand. Some of us were born to be taught, while others were born to figure it out on their own. But what's the one thing that we all need and can always benefit from? Accountability. This book is not just a tool meant to revolutionize your sales processes, it is a way to hold yourself accountable on a daily basis, over and over again.

Let's be real about everything in this book. You're not going to like some of it, but don't let that be something that hinders you from utilizing the things you do like. Make these methods and ideas *YOUR OWN*. Apply your own R.E.A.S.O.N. to everything you've read and evolve certain thoughts in a way that make you more comfortable. This is important for your future growth.

Understand there is nothing greater than your destiny. The path you travel will be remembered as the footprint you leave on this earth. And remember that there are no coincidences, rather challenges that will allow you to transcend into greatness. As the sun sets on this book, and on your adventure with us.

Do not make it the last chapter of your story.

A sunset can be compared against our earthly walk in two ways: It can be seen as the end. A forgotten story of comfort and mediocrity. Or, it can be remembered as your Legend. A Legacy of *EPIC* proportions. One that cannot be put into a box or dumbed down into a statement, but one that causes intrigue, curiosity, and an insatiable desire to know more. One that transcends perceptions and changes the game in every moment it encounters. Not just for you, but for the community who has latched onto it and will never forget the ways in which you've impacted them.

When my father passed, at his celebration of life, my family and I had been sitting in the front row of the room. Overwhelmed with emotion and not paying much attention to anything but our own sorrow and grief, I rose up from my seat to give some words in remembrance of my Hero. As I settled at the podium, I looked out across the room for the first time. There had to be a thousand people in attendance, standing, sitting, still walking in through the doors. It was an overwhelming feeling. At that moment, I suddenly realized just how big the impact my father had on his community. People came up to me afterward (for hours) telling me all the things they loved about my father. Some from his childhood, some college buddies, some of my friends even.

But the best... the people who told me "your dad sold me my copier."

I had an awakening that day. My father never separated who he was from his work... because his work was to care for and be involved in his community. You might have seen them as his customers, but he saw them as his family.

And so, remember to walk this earth as a Servant Leader to all those you encounter. It, in turn, will cause a tiny spark. One that turns into a glorious blaze. And as the sun sets on your journey, know that it does not have to be the end. Indeed, for the lion-hearted, it is only your beginning.

TAKE A FEW MOMENTS AND REFLECT ON THE QUOTE AT THE BEGINNING OF THE DAY...

TODAY'S ADVENTURE

Take a moment and honor those you have lost during your time on this earth. Whether it is physical death, a lost relationship, or a separation of any sort. Remember that our time is short, so our actions must be intentional and transcend the way the world would define the right kind of response. If this person I am directing you to honor has harmed you, forgive them. If you feel lost and broken without them, celebrate them. This kind of focus will allow for the type of personal development needed in order to become a Legend during your own walk, and will set a new example for the coming generations. Use this space to collect your thoughts...

_____

_____

_____

_____

_____

_____

_____

_____

DAY 30

SUNSETS AND LEGENDS

A PAINTING IN MY FATHERS' OFFICE

"On the plains of hesitation, bleach the bones of countless millions, who on the verge of victory sat down to rest, and while resting died."

It has been an absolute pleasure to spend these last 30 days with you. To show you the success The Copier Warrior has experienced through Rebellion, to challenge the status quo of the sales world alongside you. I believe in your success, and the abilities you possess in your unique makeup.

Remember, it's not easy to be your own individual in a world that prefers you to conform to its standards. I have always wondered who gets to set those standards... my conclusion?

It's you, and only you, who will change the course you are on. Starting as a thought, evolved into a spark, and ending with the world on fire.

On this final day, it is important to look back and realize all that you've accomplished. This has not been an easy journey, but, hopefully, it has been rewarding. Sales is ultimately about leading yourself, and, if you've finished this book, you've done an excellent job thus far.

Today, put the focus on yourself and your community — the new culture of friendship that you've developed, your growing ability to relate with others on a personal level, your newfound Living Pipeline, your R.E.A.S.O.N. your Roots, your Chest of Wonder, and how you've done all this in only 30 days. You should, without a doubt, be incredibly proud of what you've done!

And, while you've finished the book, we urge you to recognize that this is only the beginning. You are now equipped with some basic tools and insights that will differentiate you from the majority of salespeople. Make them your own and go forth — good and faithful servant.

The foundations of Rebellion have now been etched into stone. Your stone...

The Copier Warrior has been laid to rest and the mantle has been handed to you. Now, go and sell as you've never sold before.

TAKE A FEW MOMENTS AND REFLECT ON THE QUOTE AT THE BEGINNING OF THE DAY...

TODAY'S ADVENTURE

Start a Sales Rebellion!

IT IS TIME. RISE OH REBEL AND BECOME YOUR OWN LEGEND.

DAILY ADVENTURES:

- [ ] **D1**: Create your mission statement
- [ ] **D2**: Log your A, B, and C accounts
- [ ] **D3**: Have a conversation rather than pitching them
- [ ] **D4**: Practice some customer care
- [ ] **D5**: Engage in experiential learning and industry knowledge
- [ ] **D6**: Decide and sign
- [ ] **D7**: Give something away
- [ ] **D8**: Write down your habits and create a new schedule
- [ ] **D9**: Create a targeted list of 10% of your overall list
- [ ] **D10**: Curate your list on LinkedIn

- [ ] **D11**: Categorize local networking groups and join one
- [ ] **D12**: Begin learning your tools — EDC, Google Alerts, etc.
- [ ] **D13**: Reflect and Reconnect
- [ ] **D14**: Give something away again
- [ ] **D15**: Eat lunch with strangers
- [ ] **D16**: Start building your Living Pipeline
- [ ] **D17**: Start building your Chest of Wonder
- [ ] **D18**: Pick some strategic referral partners
- [ ] **D19**: Meet the receptionist and HR Manager
- [ ] **D20**: Decide on the most important piece for your future

- [ ] **D21**: Go the extra mile and experience what it's like
- [ ] **D22**: Go hard at closing time — Call on someone "after hours"
- [ ] **D23**: Explore your prospect's territory — The one within
- [ ] **D24**: Awaken a prospect with a Delta Moment
- [ ] **D25**: Begin your leadership journey
- [ ] **D26**: Sharpen your street cred with product knowledge
- [ ] **D27**: Redefine failures and change perceptions
- [ ] **D28**: Honor your legacy
- [ ] **D29**: Honor those you are separated from
- [ ] **D30**: Start a Sales Rebellion

SALES

REBEL

**Co -founder
& CSO**

Dale
Dupree

**AKA: Copier
Warrior**

+1 (407) 719-2844

Dale@thesalesrebellion.com

knoxville, TN

ABOUT ME

I'm on a mission to help sales teams Rebel against "typical" sales results... Sell More... Suck Less...
Become a Sales Rebel!

Specializations

Sales + Marketing

Personal Branding

Sales Culture

Sales Leadership

LEARN MORE:

SALES

REBEL

Co -founder & CEO

Jeffery Villegas

AKA: El Jefe

+1 (423) 994-4542

Jeff@thesalesrebellion.com

Orlando, FL

ABOUT ME

I'm on a personal mission to change the way people think about the world by challenging beliefs and assumed identities.

Specializations

Transformational
Leadership

Organizational
Culture

Systems & Process

Communication
Science

LEARN MORE:

Printed in Great Britain
by Amazon

41690024R00096